THE CITIZEN

THE CITIZEN

A Study of the Individual and the Government

BY

Nathaniel Southgate Shaler

Professor of Geology in Harvard University, and Dean of Lawrence Scientific School

New York
A. S. Barnes and Company
1904

Copyright, 1904
BY A. S. BARNES & COMPANY

Published February, 1904
Second Printing, June, 1904

PREFACE

IT is commonly supposed by those who have to do with young people that they cannot be brought to understand large matters relating to the management of public affairs, which are cared for by our government in its various forms of town, county, state, and national authorities. My own belief, based on many years' experience as a teacher, leads me to the conviction that this view is quite mistaken: that so far from being unfitted to deal with such questions, young men and women are naturally interested in knowing those things which pertain to their duties in the wide field of life upon which they are entering. Therefore it is with some confidence that I have determined to set forth in the following pages the leading facts concerning the relations of the citizens of this country — men and women alike — to the systems of the society and the government in which we all have to play our part. Large as are the questions which have to be dealt with, they are made the easier to understand by the fact that they are ever before us, as part of our life.

The aim of this book is to set before the reader the relation which the individual bears to the government which controls his conduct as a citizen. In beginning this task it is most desirable to bring clearly to mind the manner in which each of us, in our time, is introduced into human society. For some years after our career in this world is begun we know little or nothing of human relations beyond the narrow circle of the households in which we belong, the schools we attend, or the friendships which we may form. All the experience of life which we thus gain is accepted as a matter of course, as we accept the fact that we are alive. Sometime between the twelfth and sixteenth year the mind in its natural growth awakens to larger understandings; we begin to see that the relations of men, like the other features of this world, are exceedingly complicated, and that some study is required to make them in any measure plain.

The awakening and enlargement of the mind, which should come with the passage from infancy to young womanhood or manhood, is not experienced by all. It unfortunately happens with many persons that the body and the motives which relate to it develop without a corresponding growth of the spiritual nature. Such people remain, so far as their understanding goes, mere children, who hinder and have to be cared for by those who are so fortunate as to attain the normally grown-up state of mankind. In many instances this failure to attain the fit growth of the intelligence doubtless arises from the fact that when at the age in which the mind naturally turns from the interests of childhood to larger questions, the youths were not led to consider such matters, but were allowed to occupy themselves altogether with those things which were trifling. A capacity to grow to the fulness of moral and intellectual vigour has to be born in us; it is in large measure inherited from our ancestors, as are the qualities of our bodies, — their strength or weakness, their liability to disease or their ability to keep wholesome. But as we often see how a frail child may, if well cared for, become an able-bodied youth, so one who does not strongly tend to mental growth in the developing age may, by the proper use of his powers, be led to broaden his mind. For this enlargement no other studies appear to be so well adapted as those which concern the affairs of men, such as we are here undertaking.

It is not at once that the youth acquires the sense of his position in the world which makes him fit for the duties of the citizen, and thus confers on him the quality of civilised manhood: it is but slowly that he attains these understandings. They come as he considers the ways in which men do their associated work. To see, in part at least, the way in which mankind has done, and is now doing, the deeds which make up the sum of human life, it is only necessary to open our eyes and behold what is going on about us. The facts are, indeed, so simple apparently, so common, that they appear to be not worth noticing; but the student, here as elsewhere, has to learn that familiar events, when well understood, often tell us the most concerning the truths we need to know. There is a capital instance of this in the history of our understanding of gravitation: for ages men knew very well that all the solid bodies about them were heavy, that they were drawn towards the earth; but it was not until Isaac Newton found the law of this action, and showed us how it kept the earth in its course around the sun and the planets in their places, that we came to know how much the simple fact of objects falling may, if well understood, make clear.

CONTENTS

CHAPTER	PAGE
I. THE ORIGIN OF MANKIND	1
II. THE BEGINNINGS OF GOVERNMENT	15
III. WHAT LIBERTY IS	26
IV. ON THE SHARE OF THE AVERAGE MAN IN THE STATE	44
V. THE PRACTICE OF CITIZENSHIP	64
VI. CITIZENSHIP AND PARTY ALLEGIANCE	85
VII. ON THE LIMITS OF FREEDOM	103
VIII. THE CITIZEN AND THE LAW	120
IX. WEALTH — ITS ORIGIN AND DISTRIBUTION	152
X. EDUCATION, PUBLIC HEALTH, AND OTHER QUESTIONS	173
XI. IMMIGRATION, UNIVERSAL SUFFRAGE, AND THE NEGRO QUESTION	200
XII. FOREIGN POSSESSIONS	239
XIII. THE CITIZEN AND CITY GOVERNMENT	261
XIV. THE CITIZEN AND HIS FELLOW-MAN	287
XV. THE VALUE OF GREAT MEN TO THE CITIZEN	301
XVI. THE FUTURE OF THE COMMONWEALTH	331
INDEX	341

THE CITIZEN

CHAPTER I

THE ORIGIN OF MANKIND

THE student of citizenship, whether as a youth he is trying to understand his own place in the world, or as an adult man he is endeavouring to see into the problems of the society he has to help, does best to begin his inquiry by studying certain lessons which modern science has taught us concerning the origin and nature of man. These teachings rest upon a great accumulation of learning of which only the merest outlines are needed or can be given in these pages. The main point of it all is that the man of to-day is not a creature of this day, but has been gradually shaped, in the succession of his ancestors, to the state of mind and body which he now exhibits. The records of history enable us to trace our forefathers back to a time about three thousand years ago, when our Germanic stock was hardly more civilised than were the American Indians when they were first seen by Europeans. At that stage our ancestors were barbarians, just rising above the level of savagery. Still farther back, we have reason to believe that these people were yet more lowly in their nature and their habits of life: in a condition in which they knew nothing of the use of the metals, and when their only tools and utensils were made of stone, wood, bone, and baked clay. In this primitive state, the records which the historian explains leaves the northern Aryan people, the stock to which we belong, in their ancient dwelling-place about the Baltic Sea. In the same way the other great groups of men — the Semitic, including the Jews and the Turanian, which includes the Chinese — are known to have been, though somewhat longer ago, in a like unadvanced condition. Thus history shows us that the best peoples of to-day have come forth from a primitive state, where their life was very brutal.

Great as is the story of the advance of mankind which is told by the records, there are yet more important facts which the study of Natural History reveals. The inquiries of naturalists have made it evident that the body and the mind of men came forth from the lower animals. Every bone, muscle, and other part which is found in our frames exists also in the bodies of the lower creatures, such as the chimpanzee and gorilla. Step by step we may follow the stages of development of our frames from the simpler animals. Although we cannot trace every step in the long journey, we are now compelled to believe that our life began in the early history of the earth, and that what we are is the result of changes

THE ORIGIN OF MANKIND

which have led onward and upward, through the successions of parent and child, and from species to species, during a time which is perhaps to be measured by hundreds of millions of years.

While the fact that man is here to-day is to be explained by the supposition that he has come forth from the lower life, the way in which the advance has been brought about is not yet clear. It is, however, evident that in the ancestry of our species, below the human level, the upward going was largely due to the frequent occurrence of advantageous changes in the young of each generation, and that the fortunate possessors of these betterments lived on, in turn, to advance the life on its destined way, while the less happy perished.

The studies of Charles Darwin and a host of other naturalists have shown us that the lower life of the world is, and has always been, involved in a struggle for existence. Large as the world appears to us, it is always overcrowded by the animals and plants which seek an opportunity to live. Every year many more individuals come forth from seed or egg than can find a chance of attaining their growth; of these creatures those only which have some peculiar fitness for the work they need to do live on and propagate their kind; their progeny, in turn, are likely to inherit the qualities which caused their parents to survive. To this struggle for existence and the resulting survival of the fittest, we must, in the present state of our knowledge, in some measure attribute the upward going of life, which led at length to the creation of mankind.

Such, in very brief, is what is known of the history of the animal man. His body has been brought to its shape by a long battle with the difficulties of this world; by a battle through the ages in which those creatures which were the best fitted for action survived and passed their qualities onward and upward to others of higher grade. In this succession, which led in the end to man, there were many thousand stages, each represented by what is termed a species, or a group of beings as like to each other as are the individuals of the various kinds of animals we see about us.

If it were possible to recall to life all the creatures of old through which our life has found its way, from the lowest upward, arranging them in a long procession, we would note, as the column passed in review, a gradual transition from lower to higher, from simple to complex, slowly leading from creatures so simple that they seemed scarcely animate to the perception of man. We would behold how each of the myriad perfections which make up the human body has been slowly and persistently contrived, every one of them requiring ages and innumerable lives for its completion. Supposing such a procession to exhibit only these animals which were our ancestors, those alone which attained success in the en-

THE ORIGIN OF MANKIND

deavour for advancement, a thousand years might be too short a time for the train moving at the speed of a marching army to pass before us.

It is the object of the naturalists of to-day to reconstruct the history of life by searching the rocks which were made during the successive stages of the past. In these strata are found vast quantities of fossils, the remains of the beings which lived when the beds were forming as muds and sands on the bottoms of the ancient lakes and seas. This search into the crust of the earth for the records of ancient species, though it has been going on for more than a century, has been hardly more than begun. Yet it has shown us many thousand links in the chain of life, leading from the earliest times to the present day, from the simplest to the most complicated life. In this succession we behold the train of advancements which leads to man, not of course with the completeness of our imagined procession, but sufficiently so to make it clear that the train of life, from beginning to end, was unbroken. Each new discovery serves but to make more certain the mighty truth that the origin of man is to be traced downward through the host of living beings, the past dwellers on this earth, who by their divinely guided strivings have won us our place in the world.

At first sight this revelation as to the ancient history of our race, which science has given us, seems to many people very disagreeable; they dislike the idea that even in a remote way their lives are derived from the lower brutal creatures. The old view, based upon the literal acceptation of the allegory, in which in the Bible the creation of man is described, is naturally dear to us, because it long was unhesitatingly believed — any doubt as to its exact truth was taken to indicate a disbelief in the principles of the Christian religion. This state of mind has in most part passed away. Few, if any, scholarly men now hold that there is any essential relation between the statements of the ancient leader of Israel concerning the beginning of the world and the teachings of Christ; moreover, the essence of all true religion rests upon a perfect confidence in the Supreme Power that rules this world and the realms about it. Where we find the truth it must be accepted as a part of the divine order which it is our duty to understand and to make our own.

When we, apart from any prejudice, consider the scientific revelation as to the origin of man, we see in that teaching something far more stately than the old view which made him the result of a momentary exercise of the divine power. The creative work which has led our life through the ages, through tens of thousands of varied species, through the struggles and chances of all the world's history, gives us a nobler sense of a Providence than we can possibly have if we believe that we were directly shaped from the dust of the earth. There is, indeed, no truth in nature which is so inspiring as this we are now

THE ORIGIN OF MANKIND

regarding. Properly understood, it shows us that we are no accident of this world, but the result of processes which began with the shaping of the sphere, and which were so guided that after ages of endeavour in creatures which foresaw nothing of the result, there came forth man, the last of them all, the first to lift up his eyes and praise his Maker.

So long as the life which was in the end to take shape in man was in the stages below his level, the conditions of the intelligence were very different from what they became when the human stage was won. In the lower creations we find intelligence in certain ways like our own. If we observe active-witted animals, such as dogs, monkeys, or elephants, either in their wild or trained state, we readily note that they think and are guided by their thoughts, much as we ourselves are guided. There is reason to believe that they contrive; love their friends; hate their enemies; are, in a word, affected by their experiences much as are men. It is thus evident that man brought with him, from his lower life into his higher state of being, the greater number of the qualities which constitute his mind. It is, however, clear that certain of the higher spiritual features of mankind are entirely peculiar to his kind. The religious sense, that motive which leads men to recognise in the world about them the action of a supreme, controlling intelligence, is apparently unknown in the lower life.

So, too, men in a most important way differ from the brutes in the fact that they are able to progress in their moral and intellectual growth with a rapidity which is unexampled in their lower kindred. We see this when we compare the changes which have taken place in the domesticated animals that have been captives of mankind for thousands of years. These animals, such as the horse, the sheep, and the dog, have by care been made greatly to vary in their bodies; but their minds have remained essentially unchanged, except so far as they may have lost something of their original wildness. While these companions of man have remained, as regards their minds, much as they were when in their wilderness state, their master has gone on with wonderful swiftness in a development which has carried him, in moral and intellectual qualities, very far up in the scale of being. Between the primitive, brutal savage, with hardly more moral quality than the beasts he hunted, and the conscientious, developed, moral citizen of our latter civilisations, there has been an advance in its importance to be compared with all that has been accomplished in the course of the long procession from the beginnings of life to the plane of the lowest men.

In the natural history of man, as modern science has displayed it, we see the most instructive spectacle which this earth affords. We behold a gradual advance in the qualities of mind and body, slowly

THE ORIGIN OF MANKIND

gained through the ages, until the human shape was attained; then with amazing suddenness a going forth into the realm of freedom and of duty. Those of us who properly read the lessons of this ancient history of man may find in it much that helps us to understand the meaning of our own lives as well as the problems of government which arise from the social and political associations of mankind. Perhaps the most important point that is made clear to us by the new science concerns the value of the individual life. It is clear that each step in the advance which served to place us on the earth has been effected by the efforts of the creatures which strove energetically to overcome difficulties which beset them, and, by taking advantage of the powers which came to them as individuals, succeeded in placing their race above their weaker kindred, thus winning a step upward towards the higher life. All we have that lifts us above the lowliest creatures is evidently due to the energetic efforts of individual beings, each in its time acting up to the full measure of the powers which had been granted to it. Vigorous action that called for all the inborn capacities of the being has been the condition of all advances, both before and after the coming of man.

As we pass from the lower life to the state of man, we note certain great changes in the way in which the mind, especially in its moral qualities, does its work. In the lower creatures, the selfish propensities, the individual greeds and rages, act in an unrestrained way. The animal usually loves and cares for its offspring; it has a certain affection, it may be, for the members of the herd in which it dwells; in some rare cases it will defend or care for any one of its species, but in general the only care is for itself. Such is the case also with the brutal man. The hunger and fury of the beast from which he came is strongly implanted in his spirit; but the love and self-devotion and reasoning power which were absent or narrowly limited in his brutal ancestors, and which grew but slowly in them, now vigorously spring upward, gain some measure of control of conduct, and prepare the being for civilisation.

The point to which we have now attained in this brief study as to the natural history of man enables us to see how important to the student of government is this knowledge, as to the ways in which his kind came upon this earth. We see how the lower creatures, with which we are most familiar, — the domesticated animals, — have their nature determined by that of their ancestors. We may thus judge of the controlling influence of the inheritances which each living being has as its guides in life; and also how very far primitive men, or even those of to-day, are affected by the qualities which they inherit from the lower beings, whence they came. In fact, the life of each one of us is full of ancient evil, derived from the brutes, which is ever at war with the better and

THE ORIGIN OF MANKIND

higher qualities, — the true human part of our minds. By no means all that has come to us from the lower life is evil; much of it, indeed, is, when joined with the larger affections and understandings which belong to us as men, of the best our nature affords. But in the conduct of our individual lives, as well as in the control of our societies, we have always to remember that we have in us this mingling of the old and the new life.

It is most important that the student of society and of government should see and reflect on the position of man in relation to the lower life, for in that history is to be found the basis for a true understanding of the greater part of the evils with which the reformers are ever contending, — evils which make the business of securing a good government so very difficult.

Our truly human quality points the way of life towards high places, but the ancient brutal motives are ever ready to drag men down to lower deeds, those which were fit enough for the animals, but which to men are a degradation.

Among the marvels of man's nature and history we must count as the greatest the fact that in what seems to have been his first distinctly human course of conduct he began to subjugate his brutal propensities, submitting them to the control of the higher motives of his nature. The social order of even the lowest society of savages shows us something of the sacrifice of animal greeds to the ideal of a government which shall shelter and protect the members of the community. Thence on to the highest results yet attained by our societies. All advance has been effected by the progressive increase in the power of the better human qualities in controlling actions, and by a corresponding reduction of the share which the inherited brutal motives have in the lives of men. At present in all well-ordered societies those persons who by some ill chance have not attained enough of the truly human spirit to master their animal propensities are regarded as idiots or criminals, and are put apart from their more fortunate brethren.

In the advance of living creatures all the members of a society do not go forward together. The establishment of each profitable innovation was effected by some individual born with peculiar powers and the desire to use them. In human associations the leader goes forward, and the throng follows him. This is as true in the great states of our time as in the primitive tribes of the lower races of men. Each brave, discerning person who sees some chance of improving the state or mankind, and resolutely strives for it, leads his people on the upward path. Whether his work consists in some serviceable invention, in the establishment of honest methods in public affairs, or in the discernment of a higher truth in the field of science or religion, his leadership is alike good. Its nature rests upon the anciently established principle

THE ORIGIN OF MANKIND

that all advance depends on the coming of the masterful individual who shall show the body of his kind their appointed way.

The exceptional nature of man's history, as compared with that of all other animals in past ages, consists in the very great change in his mental quality without any considerable alteration in the characteristics of his body. For all the great variety we find in men as regards their moral and intellectual character, they are in form so far alike that, notwithstanding the diversities of colour and shape, many naturalists who have given attention to the matter regard them all as of the same species; the different races, as the negro, the Indian, the Chinese, the Caucasian, being counted as mere varieties of the same stock. In fact, the body of man appears to be essentially unalterable, while his spirit is endowed with a very great capacity for change.

Although it will be profitable to the reader to make a careful study concerning the relation of mankind and the lower creatures, we have for our purpose to limit the inquiry to the statements which have been made in this chapter. The main points are that the body of man, with all its manifold parts and functions, has come to him through the lower creatures, and that his mind has in large part been derived from the same realm; the higher of its qualities having been taken on since the human state was attained. The result of this humanising process is a nature so distinct from the brute ancestors in its spiritual quality that we must reckon it as in a new realm, — one quite apart from that which contains the lower life. It may at first sight seem puzzling that man is here spoken of as at once very closely akin to the brutes, yet widely separated from them, but such combinations of relations and differences are very common in this world. Thus the chemist sees at every stage of his work that some slight addition to a combination of elements may entirely alter a compound. A difference in temperature too slight to be measured can change substances, such as water, from the liquid to the frozen or solid state, or in other cases may bring about a change such as the explosion of gunpowder. The question whether a seed is to grow or to decay may likewise be determined by inconceivably slight amounts of moisture and heat. In fact, this world is full of just such delicately poised conditions, in which very slight alterations of action bring about very great changes in the course of events. A century plant may develop for years until it has attained the stage at which it is prepared to put forth for flower and seed. So in a larger way it seems to have been with the coming of man. The work of the millions of years before this earth saw its master may be accounted as a period of preparation. When all was made ready the human nature began to unfold like a blossom.

CHAPTER II

THE BEGINNINGS OF GOVERNMENT

IN this chapter we shall consider the beginnings of government as they are shown in the present state of those peoples which are just entering on the paths of advancement upon which our race has travelled so far. The history of our own and of other civilised folk shows that they have slowly passed from a savage state to their present station. A host of tribes have, fortunately for our information, retained that lowly condition, so that we can from them determine how our own ancestors began their upward march.

The lowest savages show us, what we know full well from our individual experience, that man, compared with the more vigorous brutes, as regards his body is a very weak creature. His frame has little to commend it for the rough uses of this world. While his lower kinsmen are clothed with hair or wool, so as to fit the climate in which they belong, he is naked; while they have weapons for attack or defence, hoofs, strong teeth, or claws, he is unprovided with natural weapons. Moreover, owing to the fact that he has been compelled to use his forelimbs for other purposes, he has but one pair of legs for motion; the result being that nearly every large animal of the wilderness can easily outrun him. The strength of man lies not in his body but in his mind; in his intelligence, his capacity to plan actions in relation to his needs, in his quick sympathy with his fellows, and his understanding of the world about him. Beginning as a weak animal, man made head against the dangers and trials of the wilderness by his inventive power, which enabled him to make weapons and other tools. The spear tipped with a flake of stone, such as flint, gave him a better weapon than any claw or horn affords. The bow and arrow, which came later, enabled him to strike deadly blows from a distance. The possession of fire, another distinctively human acquisition, made it possible to provide utensils of baked clay and to obtain better food. These and other similar resources which nearly all savages command begin the institution of property, and on this possession of wealth rests, in a large measure, the development of all the subsequent growth of society.

The first distinct step towards civilisation after the beginning of the invention of weapons, tools, and utensils, one of enduring importance, consisted in the development of the family. On this depends the care of children, and consequently the very life of the people. It is impossible in this writing to trace in any detail the interesting history of the

BEGINNINGS OF GOVERNMENT

family relations. Beginning on a grade little, if at all, above the level of the beasts, it appears in many cases to have come to depend upon some form of marriage, in which the woman was often a captive stolen from some neighbouring tribe; she was usually regarded as, in a way, a slave, yet with certain definite privileges, which were often considerable, as in the case of the women of certain tribes of American Indians, where the wives had a right to determine on the question of making war.

The family, from the time of its origin, has been the unit by which societies have been organised; it afforded the beginning of the associations among men which led first to the tribe and then slowly to the state. The natural affection of parents and children extended to other and more remote kindred, so that larger societies were formed, all the members of which reorganised a common bond of kinship. Thus the tribe was in effect an enlarged household, more or less under the control of the chief in the beginning elder of the clan. The sense of mutual obligation, based on common ancestry, is among most primitive folk very strong, as is shown by the frequent custom of adopting the esteemed stranger by some ceremony which indicates a mixing of his blood with that of the people who admit him to their ranks. To address an Indian politely, in the manner of his people, he must be called by words which mean elder brother or younger brother, all relations being with them dependent on kinship. If the reader will compare this form of addressing the stranger with that we are accustomed to use, he will note an instructive difference. We use the terms *sir* or *mister* both alike, indicating a formal confession that the stranger is a man of authority and station, but in no way denoting any blood relationship. This apparently trifling difference in the forms of courtesy has a great meaning; for it shows a state of mind that makes possible the growth of the state to a size in which the idea of kinship of blood is lost, and in its place is set the idea of relative station.

As soon as the tribe, by the efforts of its abler men, gained in strength, it began that system of war with other tribes which is the mark of the savage state, and which has commonly persisted even among civilised peoples. So long as men were fed by the chase, which they usually did until a long time after the tribal life began, the strife for hunting grounds was the source of constant wars. Among most of these primitives peoples some form of slavery was common, and war was the natural means of winning captives. Moreover, war is but another form of hunting; it was a primitive, brutal amusement much indulged in for the scalps and heads which might be won, for the excitement which it afforded in the preliminary dances or the feasts which crowned success. In a certain measure war was an advantage in laying the foundations of the early states. The stronger tribes — those containing the ablest men, those who could contrive the best weapons and lead the warriors most successfully on their expeditions — supplanted the weaker. It acted to select the abler of the innumerable primitive tribes for control, and so continued that principle of the survival of the fittest which had operated in the lower life to lift the beings towards the level of man.

The father in the tribal state of man was not only ruler of his family, but, in most cases, he was also priest; he led in the sacrifices and other religious ceremonies. In time, and in most cases early in the development of the people, the religious functions came to be allotted to particular men. Yet priestly authority was and is often retained as a part of chieftainship among very advanced states. Julius Cæsar, by birth a man of high estate, was in early youth made pontifex maximus, a religious title making him the recognised head of the churches of his country. Such spiritual headship is also, in a certain way, claimed for the sovereigns of Russia and Great Britain.

Among all early or primitive peoples we find some recognition of powers unseen but influential on the life of man. Savages, like better-instructed people, try to shape ideas of the unseen forces which lead to natural actions. There are two usual ways in which they seek to explain such matters; in one of these the forces of nature are supposed to be due to the action of unseen animals. Thus a common Indian explanation of the wind is that the air is moved by the wings of a great, invisible bird. The idea of these mysterious animals controlling the actions of nature arises from the fact that the savage hunter is constantly experiencing the strength and skill of the creatures he hunts; he thinks much of them and is disposed to exaggerate their powers. Another common explanation of the actions that go on in the world is the supposition that they are due to the ghosts of the dead of his tribe, — men of strength in their time who, after life, remain powerful for good or evil. Various other beings, such as fairies, elves, and giants, are also supposed to people the unseen world, occasionally showing themselves to man. These creatures of fancy are believed by savages and half-civilised men to be constantly interfering with man, sometimes for good, but more commonly for evil, bringing ill fortune in the chase or in war, drought, storms, earthquakes, and other natural accidents as well as all diseases, and, in the end, death.

It is difficult to imagine how much the savage and even some apparently civilised men suffer from this superstition concerning the ways in which the world is ruled. Among such people a large part of their thought is devoted to the task of defeating the efforts of evil spirits and to soliciting the help of the good. It is not surprising that a class of men becomes

BEGINNINGS OF GOVERNMENT 21

established among these deluded people, such as the medicine-men of the Indians or the wizards of our own ancestors, whose business it was to see to the means by which the good and evil spirits may be controlled. The sufferer from disease was subjected to cruelties and even to death in order to expel the demon which was supposed to possess him. Among some savage tribes, as, for instance, in our American Indians, the loss of life from this cause was very great, perhaps greater than from their frequent wars. There can be no question that next after war superstition and the accompanying sorcery was the most oppressive evil of early peoples. In certain ways it was the greatest of all curses, for the reason that it might fall upon every man, woman, and child of the community. At any moment a person might be found guilty of being possessed of a demon for which the treatment was usually a painful death.

The doctrines of the Christian religion properly interpreted should have banished these grave superstitions from the greater part of the world, but the fact that witchcraft was punished, that half-insane women were executed by upright, God-fearing American churchmen, because they were supposed to be possessed by the devil, shows that the highest religious motives were incompetent to overcome this monstrous error. The only way out of this slavery, in certain ways the most shameful that men have been subjected to, was through the revelations of science, which replaced the old notion of a world controlled by a mob of contending good and evil spirits by that of a world guided by the action of uniform laws. This great task of explaining things in the scientific way began with the ancient Egyptians; more than four thousand years ago it was extended thence to the Greeks, but this understanding was lost with the downfall of the Greek civilisation, and was not in a fair way to be restored until within the last three centuries. There are traces of the old superstition left even in the most civilised and educated communities, but it has ceased to be a serious evil among the better-informed peoples.

It is not easy to estimate the importance of the process of clearing away the ancient superstitious view of nature to the development of man. The true ideal of personal liberty on which all the better life of men depends could not be established until this oppression was removed. Therefore the development of natural science was a condition on which real freedom depended. Under the earlier conditions men whose lives were passed in superstitious fear were naturally fit to be enslaved by their political masters.

One other among the many conditions which made for progress towards civilisation was the development of the right to hold property. With the lowest savages the idea of property was very limited; there

BEGINNINGS OF GOVERNMENT 23

was, indeed, little to which the notion could be applied. At first the man's sense of possessions concerned alone his arms, clothing, and ornaments. There was no individual ownership in land; even the food was a common store from which each member of the society could take sufficient for his needs. Gradually, as the tribe began to depend on agriculture, the fields for tillage were each year allotted for use on some basis of division by families. In course of time the title to land, which originally was supposed to belong to the chief, as the representative of the tribe, came to be more or less completely in the hands of the tiller of the soil. Yet in some countries the plan of common ownership is to this day retained.

With the development of the arts individuals or families began to have more personal property than at first existed; flocks and herds became important possessions; the invention of the loom gave stores of cloth; every art, indeed, added to wealth and served to develop questions as to property rights. In the old tribal state the tribe itself or the chieftain as its representative was supposed to have a kind of right to all the goods of his people; but the more men came to have of value, the more the notion of individual rights began to be asserted, and so the development of distinct property law began.

Some notions of justice serving to guide the chiefs or head men in their decisions concerning wrongs done by one person to another appears to have been in existence from the very beginnings of tribal life. Such injuries were commonly atoned for by payments of various kinds made by the offender. So that an idea of property existed even before wealth began to accumulate, but it is to the extension of personal possessions, which began when men abandoned the habit of living by the chase alone, and betook themselves to tilling the earth, or to flocks and herds, that we must attribute the development of property law.

The development of property served to create in man that idea of fixed rights and rules in the conduct of human affairs which has made civilisation possible. The idea of absolute right, at first well established in relation to possessions, was in time naturally and easily extended to matters pertaining to personal liberty. In this way the original despotic authority of the chief or king over the bodies and lives of his people became in time limited. At first all these rules of conduct were traditional; but as soon as the arts of writing were invented, as they were in one or another form among all the peoples which attained to civilisation, they were generally recorded, and became the treasures of the states which were so fortunate as to possess them. So important was this record of the law that we may fairly assume that a people entered on the plane of civilisation when they had attained in their social

BEGINNINGS OF GOVERNMENT

development to the point when their laws were written down.

We have now glanced at a few of the most important steps which have to be taken in order to lift the primitive animal man up the ways that lead towards civilisation. At each step in the advance of a people the system of government under which they live profoundly affects their welfare; it may, if it is fit, serve to help them on their way upward, as has long been the case with the government of the English-speaking peoples, or it may tend to lessen the energy and courage of men, so that they make no progress in the arts of life, as is the case with countries which are under the Mohammedan governments.

The first condition of a government is that it shall be so ordered that while it secures the most complete protection to the lives and property of the people, it shall leave the largest possible freedom to the individual. This ideal of liberty is slowly developed; it is, in fact, the latest product of advance in government, one that is just now, after centuries of active discussion and contest, taking shape. This matter of liberty — its nature, limits, rights, and responsibilities — is so hard to understand and so important to a right view concerning the place of the citizen, that we shall have to give it careful consideration; it is the proper subject of the next chapter.

CHAPTER III

WHAT LIBERTY IS

THE idea of liberty is very ancient. Nevertheless, it is not yet clear to the masses of men what liberty or freedom means or should mean to the citizen. To clear up this point we must attend to certain features in the history of man's relation to government which have already been referred to in the foregoing brief account of the steps which led from savagery to civilisation.

In the early state of mankind the common man was practically a slave to the head of his family or to the chief who was the head of the enlarged family, the clan. He was brought up to feel himself a subject, one who had hardly any rights that his superiors were bound to respect. Much is said in fanciful writings concerning the freedom of the savage. The fact is that slavery of an abject kind is the lot of all men in primitive societies; they are slaves to their chiefs and to an endless array of superstitions and customs. Gradually, with the development of wealth, and of the law which comes therewith, the man began to consider his rights; very slowly he gained an idea of his own value as an independent being. The slow-

WHAT LIBERTY IS

ness with which this value of the man to himself, of his right and duty by his natural powers, was established even among abler folk, is indeed surprising.

To the men of the earlier ages the individual was felt to have value only because he belonged to some clan, state, chief, or king. The Roman's boast was not that he was a man, but that he was a Roman; and in one or another form the ancients found their right to esteem in that they belonged to some power which alone gave them their place and value. With the diffusion of knowledge concerning the nature of man's relations to the world about him, with a clearer sense as to the history of his kind, and with the broadening of the understanding as to the meaning of laws, men began to question the rights of their superiors. For thousands of years before the so-called French Revolution, the growth in the art of government had led to more and more bitter oppression of the common people. Every one in authority above them used the various means of taxation to seize upon their earnings. For all their days they were taxed in money, or labour, or their lives were given on battlefields for causes in which they had no interest. At length there came a revolt against this oppression.

There had been endless revolts all down the ages in which the people withstood tyrants, but until the middle of the eighteenth century these struggles were, except in the case of the individual able men, on the part of conquered people against their oppressors, or of the lower classes against those in authority; sometimes the cities fought the kings of the land in which they lay, or a trade association struggled, as in our time, to maintain its privileges. But these contests, in almost all instances, were for the rights of communities of men and not for those of individuals. For a long time, however, the progress of human affairs had led to a higher estimation of the citizen. Some of the features in this progress we may well note in a brief way, as follows: —

In the Middle Ages the customs of war became greatly changed from what they were in the Roman times. Men no longer fought in serried ranks, in some cases chained together, as in the later Roman battles, but separately, in such a manner that there was a place for heroism to do its part. Even the lowest man had a chance, by the display of extraordinary valour or skill, to win his way upward. The extension of education through the church and other schools, and the development of professions, also gave a chance for men of ability, even if of lowly birth, to achieve high station. The discovery of the New World—the Americas—opened wide fields for enterprising spirits where men were free to win their way to wealth and power. Even more effectively than these the advance in the understanding of the world that science has given to man made for freedom. By the growth of such knowledge it came to

WHAT LIBERTY IS

be seen that the old idea that the world was a place of mere accidents and iniquities, which was soon to be consumed in a vast burning sent as a judgment of God, was mistaken. In the place of this misconception there began to arise in the minds of abler men a sense of the nobility of human life and of the dignity of the individual man. At first this enlarged view of man's place in nature was limited to a few philosophers; it is doubtful, indeed, if the bettered understanding would have made much growth had it not been that a place had been made ready in this country where such ideas could readily take root.

The growth of the English colonies in this country gave to the men of our race the first good chance for a great experiment in individual freedom. The settlements brought together people who had the traditions of England, a country which had gone further towards the enfranchisement of men than any other land. Moreover, in the vast wilderness to which they came, each man and woman had to summon up strength and courage for the battle for life against a host of enemies. They had to subdue the earth to their uses; to shape a society; to build a civilisation by their valour and skill. All the ancient framework of authority was lacking; even the system of church government which, in the Catholic settlements of Canada or Mexico, held the people in some bondage to the Old World, was absent, or, at least, did not exist in an oppressive form in those parts of the colonies which were of Protestant-English origin, and which shared in the revolutionary movement.

The American colonies were in many ways peculiarly adapted to be the nursery of freedom not only in the sense of independence of rulers, but in the more important regard of individual liberty. Here alone, in all the history of civilised man, had there been a chance given to people of intelligence and culture to emancipate themselves from the tyranny of ancient institutions which, even in the best of the old governments, reduced each person to the place of a servant of a system. Even those of high estate, not excepting the sovereigns, were thus hampered in their actions, being in effect mere parts of a great machine. Coming to a wilderness which could be subdued to fertility, which afforded abundant opportunities for enterprise, in no wise restrained in their activities, our forefathers gradually escaped from the cramping influences of their ancient life. They became accustomed to think and act freely, guided only by the ideals which their religious and social traditions and their written law enjoined upon them. They laid the foundations of commonwealths, but the better part of their building was done in the development of individual independence.

After more than one hundred years of existence in a state of tolerable independence, the American colonies began to feel the tightening reins of authority. The mother country, at first careless of her

WHAT LIBERTY IS

far-away possessions, seeing at length that they were destined rapidly to grow, undertook to reduce them to some control, so that they might be of profit to her. The steps which were taken were, as measured by the customs of European states in reference to their colonies, of a very mild sort. To a Spanish colony the worst of the so-called British oppression would have appeared as liberty, yet they led to a determined rebellion.

It appears tolerably plain that the colonial Revolution was not so much a contention against the taxation which was laid on the people by a parliament in which they were not represented, or against the foreign governors who were sent as tokens of the imperial authority, as an unexpressed, perhaps not distinctly felt revolt against the system of privileges, castes, and other subjections of the individual man, from which the colonists had become emancipated and which they feared might again be thrust upon them. It was the sense of personal government by the well-meaning but very dull king, George the Third, that exasperated the colonists even more than the errors or oppressions of the British Parliament. In a word, the American man had been so far emancipated by his life of a hundred years in a new land, where the institutions were to a great extent of his own making, that he could not endure the methods of the old world. He became a rebel because he had outgrown the system of the mother country.

The Declaration of Independence is a clear and masterful statement of the conclusions to which the thinking people of this country had come in their long training in a large, free life. It said in a vigorous way the thoughts which had formed themselves in the minds of these men emancipated from hampering traditions, and free to consider the place of the individual in his government apart from the old bondage of customs. The key to this account of their state of mind, which our forefathers thought fit to give to the world, and which that world has well remembered, is that "all men are born free and of equal rights." Much objection has been made to this statement for the reason that it was written by a man of the slaveholding class of Virginia, and therefore has a certain element of untruth on its face. Moreover, it is not at once clear what is meant by rights, for, as is evident, the differences of capacity with which men are endowed leads in a natural and inevitable way to a great diversity in what the world may properly give them. Thus, a dull-witted youth may have no birthright to an education such as might fairly be claimed as due to one of large intellectual powers. Yet there for the first time in the history of mankind do we find this conception of the man as detached from the ancient enslaving institutions which made for his oppression in the societies.

The effect of this declaration of independence,

WHAT LIBERTY IS

though considerable in this country, has been even more marked among other peoples than our own. Here it merely embodied in apt phrases what had long been firmly set in the minds of the people, and which has ever since abided with them. In effect, the trials of the Revolutionary War and the subsequent years of political activity reduced this proclamation among the people who put it forth to the position of a revered literary monument, the reading of which was not likely to convey much inspiration to those who knew the best of it by heart before they ever heard its noble phrases.

It was otherwise in foreign countries: to many oppressed peoples, such as the Spanish colonies of America and especially to the French, the American Bill of Rights came as a revelation of political gospel. The doctrine of freedom by birth had in a way been established in England before the American Revolution. In the mother country slaves were adjudged free from the time they set foot on the soil; so, too, equal rights before the law for all except sovereigns had, long before our declaration, been effectively a part of the English system; but to the less advanced folk of continental Europe the ideas thus vigorously stated and supported by successful war had a most inspiring quality. Out of the stir which it made, or helped to make, came the French Revolution, which, beginning with fair promise, soon became a sad travesty of the doctrine of freedom, equality, and the brotherhood of man. Other political movements, in South America and Mexico, as well as in Europe, have owed much of their spirit, if not their very beginnings, to the example of our people set them in 1776, supported, as it has been, by the successes in war and peace which came in its train.

Perhaps the most important motive of freedom which animates our people and which is expressed in the Declaration and in the more effective federal Constitution has been due to the long-continued and far-reaching discussion of liberty by many able men. The discussion is indeed a very ancient matter, but among the older writers it is usually either fanciful or related to states of society or views concerning it which are unreal, if not impossible. Only since the American experiment has there been any effort made to set the nature of liberty before the people in a way to be helpful to those who are to live in the conditions of a republic such as our own. The greater number of these writings are based on the assumption that society rests on a kind of contract which has been in some way or other entered into by the citizens of a state, and which binds them together much as men are held in business engagements: that their rights in the state and their obligations to one another rest upon this agreement into which each person enters at his birth.

It cannot be denied that there are rights and obligations which bind men together in a government,

WHAT LIBERTY IS

but these elements of union are not to be reckoned as founded on any ancient agreement, for such an agreement has never existed; they rest upon the nature of mankind. If our kind could be re-created from the dust and newly set to the task of living together, social and political bonds would doubtless arise and come to be in quality as we now find them. In other words, it is from within the man, and not from without, that arise the shaping influences which make the noblest thing of this world, — the perfect citizen. Therefore, to understand the nature of liberty each man must look within himself, examine his motives, and learn how his desires have come to be what they are. He must see how the ancient animal selfishness and greed have, by the ordering of Providence through the long ancestral training, been so far subjected to the newer and better impulses that the beast and savage have given place to the religious man devoted to noble ends and willing to sacrifice himself for the good of his kind; ready to die in order to save his fellows from misery or to lift them to a higher plane of life. Let us, then, see if we can find in ourselves the qualities on which citizenship rests.

Although it is not very easy for a man to see into himself, — into his mind, wherein is recorded the most wonderful of all earthly histories, — the facts which we have to note are so plain that it requires no more than common insight to understand them.

First of these is that every person who is not an idiot, or who has not reduced himself to the state of a beast by long-continued evil doing, has a natural affection for his fellow-beings. Among the less developed of our kind, with children and savages, this love of the neighbour is limited to kindred and other persons who are well known; but with the advance in civilisation, and as a condition and test of that advance, this sympathy goes forth first to the other people of the tribe or state, then to all mankind, and, in time, still further, though as yet among but a few, to the lower creatures which with us share the blessings of life. On this love of fellow-beings who feel as we do has rested all the advance which has led us out of the ancient darkness to the modern day; on it has depended the association of individuals in societies and states for mutual help. When and in proportion as this motive is awakened, informed by religion and by the understanding, it gives the person the true citizenly motive, the desire to do under the guidance of reason those things which may best help his fellow-men.

At first among men this motive of sympathy and of self-sacrifice is weak; but as the savage goes on towards civilisation, indeed, as the cause of the advance, it becomes ever stronger and more effective in its helpfulness. So, too, in the child it is limited to those just about him, and leads to no motive of self-sacrifice; but as the youth comes to the dignity

WHAT LIBERTY IS

of manhood or womanhood this flower unfolds to give beauty and sweetness to life, in time to yield its good fruit in the citizenly quality. The mark of this growth is found in the increased interest in such things as we are now considering. The history of our kind, the problems of government and of the social order, which are beyond the comprehension of the child, but become attractive as it passes towards the adult, in fact, the true growing up of the mind and soul, is as distinctly and inevitably marked by these enlargements of the spirit as is that of the body by its increase in size and strength.

It should not be supposed that these affections for the fellow-men will perfectly develop of themselves because of what comes to us from our ancestors, or that which we insensibly take in from the life about us. Some growth of the motives is, except in very low people, sure to occur, but the fulness thereof is only to be had by the exercise of these gifts. A child may be born with a promise of health and strength, but if kept in a prison and with but enough food to maintain life it will never fulfil that promise. So, too, with the love and understanding of the fellow-beings, these offerings will perish unless sustained by their fit nourishment and exercise; the more so than those of the body, for the reason that they are not so firmly fixed in the inheritances of man. Therefore every youth should have his mind nourished by those things in the way of knowledge which will help him to know and to love his comrades of the present and the past. Such history as tells us of the self-devotion of men, which has served to make our lot good; such poetry as develops or records the high-minded endeavours of those who have striven to elevate the thoughts of their race, — all indeed that shows us how we came up from the level of the brutes to the dignity of citizens in an enduring state is needed to awaken us to the full sense of our duty by the heritage of human achievement which is committed in trust to our hands.

As the student gains in knowledge of human history, not that of princes and battles, which all too often masquerades as history, but of the love and self-sacrifice which alone have made for the ennoblement of man, he will come of his own knowledge to feel that true liberty in the largest sense rests upon the right and duty of the man to exercise the higher qualities of his intelligence for his own development, and ever for the benefit of those who may be bettered by his thoughts or deeds. He will find that many kinds of men have been considered heroic or, at least, have had the name of heroes in the common reckoning.

If he examines into the lives of these famous people, he will discover that the greater number of them have lacked the quality of freemen, in that they were slaves to their passions or to their selfish desires, and that so far from their abilities being

WHAT LIBERTY IS

profitable to their kind, their lives were a curse to humanity.

From this point of view it will be instructive for the inquirer to compare the careers of George Washington and Napoleon Bonaparte, men of the same century, alike of commanding ability, and with similar opportunities of leadership in revolutionary periods of their respective nations. The one, our own hero, gave himself with a single-hearted devotion, without thought of recompense, to the grave task of leading his people. Never taking a penny for his services as a soldier, never seeking for preferment or authority beyond the limits necessary for the performance of his obligations, he led his countrymen through many years of trial to the political freedom they coveted. Again, for eight years as their chief magistrate, he helped them to order their institutions, so that their liberty might be affirmed and secured for the generations to come. This task done, he laid down his authority and betook himself once again to the life of the planter, which he had regretfully left, in order that he might do the will of his fellow-citizens. In every trait this is the history of the ideal freeman; of the man liberated from the enslaving influence of prejudices and of greeds, and animated by an intelligent affection for his fellow-men.

Against the truly heroic figure of Washington set that of Bonaparte, doubtless the abler of the two, if ability be judged by mere mental power. Placed, like our American leader, amid a great overturning of his state, he used every opportunity that chance and his sagacity gave him to gather the strength of the tyrant. Mastering his people for his selfish purposes, for a score of years he wasted them in merciless wars, which in the end cost the lives of more men than dwelt within the limits of the United States when Washington laid down his sword as commander of the colonial armies. In this course Bonaparte's main aim was ever the increase of his personal power and fortunes, and the aggrandisement of his family; in seeking to attain these ends, no considerations of fair dealing, much less of mercy, found any place; his career ended with his country in ruins, with no profit to his people for their sacrifices, and with his worn-out body a prisoner in the hands of stronger, because freer, men. It may be granted to those of to-day who are renewing the worship of the Corsican adventurer that some improvements in the laws and other institutions of France were due to his action; it is indeed true that almost any intelligence as great as his is certain to better in some respects the mere machinery of the state which it controls; but rightly judged by the standards of liberty and the patriotism which comes therefrom, the life of that man was a curse to his time and people, the greater because of his amazing ability. Thus from a comparison of two men who

WHAT LIBERTY IS

worked together in the affairs of mankind, we see the difference between the ancient, selfish type of the tyrant enslaved by himself and the modern hero, who, freed from the bondage of greed, gives his strength for the good of his kind.

Probably no one man has ever been able to do for his country as much as Washington did in the term of his service as Commander and President. The opportunity was singularly large; it was met with courage, judgment, and self-sacrifice, yet his life is but a very noble example of what a man of fair but not great intellectual ability may do for his people if he be just, high-minded, and sympathetically devoted to their best interests. When a man thus puts aside himself he gains a power for good that no inborn talent can possibly give him, for by dismissing his greeds he becomes fitted to act in the large and free way which true patriotism requires. So long as he seeks personal ends he can win only transitory things, — goods which end with his life, — which may indeed satiate and weary him before he comes to die; but that which he does for others lives after him.

So far as our country is better than other lands, it is so because its better citizens have had the unselfish spirit of their great leader of a century ago. All our hope of maintaining its high place depends upon the succession of like citizens, who, animated with the true spirit of liberty, may ever be ready to see to it that their fellows are likewise free; who recognise that the test of freedom is the sense of duty by the neighbour, or that throng of neighbours we name the state.

It is hardly needful to say that the idea of freedom which is here presented to the reader is akin to those which enter into the Christian religion. The love of the fellow-man, the desire to help him to the enjoyment and enlargement of his life, is, in truth, at once religious and patriotic.

The great question before the people of any free state is whether they can keep the citizens in successive generations so alive to the real nature and duties of freemen that their commonwealth may be maintained in its spirit. In a despotic state, one which is fully controlled by the machinery of its government, the engine of the state may continue to work because it has been so contrived as to take account of the prevailing selfishness of men; but in a democratic republic the system reckons that a great majority of the citizens are fully imbued with the motives of freemen, and that they will ever manifest the devotion of the public good which is characteristic of those who know what true liberty is, and will consecrate themselves to its interests. As soon as a majority of the voters relapse into the condition of the folk who dwell under despotic governments, we may be sure that the state will become worse than those which are ruled in the ancient arbitrary way.

WHAT LIBERTY IS

The question, therefore, which every American citizen has to consider when he is about to enter on the grave responsibilities which are to be conferred on him is as to the ways in which he can do his share to continue and enlarge the spirit of liberty which has come to his day from the times before. Not only must he seek to perpetuate what we have of that free and dutiful spirit; he must strive to enhance it, to deepen the sense of obligation by public duty, and to bring it home to a greater proportion of the people. As with other matters of the mind, public spirit cannot remain in a fixed state; as the price of living at all, it must continue to grow. We will therefore consider what the youth of our time should endeavour to do in fostering the liberty which has been given them to cherish.

CHAPTER IV

ON THE SHARE OF THE AVERAGE MAN IN THE STATE

AS the writer well knows from the memories of his own youth, the spectacle which a young man beholds when he begins his life as a citizen is not such as is likely to encourage him to believe that he can do much to affect his country for good or ill. There are at the present time about seventy-five million people in the United States; of these about forty million are adult men and women who are effective in some measure in shaping the society or its government. Nearly twenty million have the right to vote, and thus may have an immediate share in the conduct of the government; among these hosts of what account is the life and work of one man?

The answer to this question is easily made: no person can clearly foresee what value his deeds may have to his fellow-men; his responsibility goes no further than his powers. If he acts unselfishly and to the best of his ability for the good of his comrades; if he does all he can to inspire those about

SHARE OF THE AVERAGE MAN

him to do likewise, — his duty is done; the rest he must leave to the Power above.

We should be careful to remember that public duty is made up of the personal duty of the individual members of the state. We are apt to get the notion that the commonwealth is something apart from the persons who dwell within it; only so far as each and every man and woman lives in a fit way can it be a *common wealth*. A rude but effective parallel to the place of the average man in a state is to be found in the position of a private soldier in the ranks of an army. There, as in the state, he may be one of a thousand or of millions, but his path of duty is as clear, if not clearer, than if he fought alone. He owes to himself and to his neighbours the perfect and intelligent devotion of his strength and courage as in a common cause. To the tasks before him his duty is as obligatory as though he commanded the host. His reward, in the peace of mind that comes when his conscience tells him that he has done for the best up to the measure of his capacity, is as great as that of the commander.

The analogy between the duty of the soldier and that of the citizen is defective in a way which should be pointed out, though the reader may have seen it already. The soldiers in the ranks have but to obey orders

> Theirs not to make reply;
> Theirs not to reason why;
> Theirs but to do and die."

Thus the position of all but the commander of a host has only one likeness to the attitude of the freeman; this is in the element of self-devotion which may animate them. The duty and privilege of the citizen is to reason as to his conduct and to debate all his plans of action with his neighbours. On this account the habit of the soldier, which leads to swift and unquestioning obedience, is very different from that which inspires the citizen. As the rulers of the European states well know, the best way to keep their people in safe control is to subject all the young men to military discipline in the years when habits of mind are most easily formed; they thus acquire the custom of implicit obedience to command.

In the ranks of citizens each man is essentially a commander: it is his to plan for the good of his people and to act in their behalf to the measure of his abilities; whether he be successful or no, he has enriched himself by his endeavour. Success, in some measure, is so certain to follow from any reasonable effort to better the commonwealth that we may all look forward to that reward. It must not be supposed that to do good work by the state it is necessary for a man to have the large public opportunities which are afforded by a leader's position or influence, — such men as are needed to animate and direct a people in times of grave difficulties. In absolute governments, where the people have no effective

SHARE OF THE AVERAGE MAN

share in affairs, the whole direction of the state commonly depends upon leaders, or rather rulers, but in a republic the plain citizen has to do his own thinking; he has really to direct the course of events.

So important is the work which is to be done by the plain people of this country, that if it were in our power to choose between having a hundred able statesmen created for public affairs, or of bringing into such work a hundred thousand men of ordinary life who were engaged in private business, but who would inform themselves concerning their political duties and act on that knowledge in a dutiful way, we would be compelled to select the last-named contribution, for the reason that it would be more profitable to the commonwealth. In the present condition of this country the supreme need is for a great number of men who have an understanding of liberty, its rights and obligations, and who will, by their speech and conduct, influence their neighbours to acquire a like state of mind.

Those who know the state of our society have often had chances to see how some one private citizen has, in a way unnoticed by himself and by those about him, so controlled the people of a neighbourhood that they show the effect of his mastering mind. The writer has often observed this admirable influence of some unrecognised patriot in the high grade of citizenship noticeable in a rural community where the little society was surrounded by people of a very much lower quality. The blessed difference is indicated in the way the men and women of the place look upon the questions of private and public conduct; in their devotion to those things which shape the action of the adults and to guide the youth to the right way. It is often possible to trace the good which has thus been done to its source; if this be found it is likely to be discovered in the life of some plain man who has had no recognised station as a political leader, but who has had the quality of the patriot guide in that he has seen what true liberty meant and has set it before those about him. The man may have passed away a generation or more ago, but his deeds live after him to bless his people and to enrich the state. These uncelebrated prophets of good government make the strength of the republic; all the true and faithful leaders who are in high offices are in a way their agents. As soon as our country comes to depend upon its highly placed men for guidance, it will lose its character as a democracy and descend to the level of an oligarchy, — a state in which the power does not arise from the people, but is in a selected few who, by their superiority of wealth, birth, or education, are able to control the government.

It should be noted that there is a natural tendency in every republican government to run into either of two kinds of danger: on the one hand, the uninformed, little-thinking masses of people moved by whims or prejudices, stirred, it may be, by the captivating speech of demagogues to become the tools of their greed or ambition. The result of this is certain danger to the best interests of the commonwealth. On the other hand, the people, losing the true spirit of liberty, to keep which involves much labour, carelessly leave the matters of their government in the hands of those who find their occupation and profit in public affairs. They get into the habit of following their leaders blindly; they are apt to look upon any criticism of them as disloyalty. In such a state a commonwealth is on the road towards an oligarchy, — a kind of government which is rather more dangerous to the best interests of liberty than a despotism pure and simple. These two dangers of republican institutions are not limited to the work of the state or federal government, they are equally grave in our precinct, town, city, and other local organisations; they are indeed rather more serious in those lesser parts of our machinery than in the greater.

In the present condition of our country, even in the most enlightened societies, it is too much to expect that every voter will have the ability, the training, or the innate patriotic motives which will make it possible out of his own spirit to win the support for true liberty which the commonwealth needs. The only way to preserve our institutions and to insure their advance to a higher plane is to raise up those leaders of opinion who, in all stages of human advancement, have been the most effective guides of the people. Into this army of the good every youth who sympathises with the objects here set forth may of right enter. If he takes his place and fills it manfully, he will have as his reward the assurance that he is thereby serving his country as nobly and to as good purpose as he could have done on any battlefield or in any legislative hall. To fit himself for the place of a leader of his people it is requisite that the youth should gain a clear idea as to the history of human society and the ways in which it does its work. A general account as to how peoples came to the exalted stage of civilisation has been presented in the foregoing pages.

It now remains to set forth in outline the ways in which our own system of government operates, its advantages and defects, and the manner in which the patriot may work to better its action. It is clear that the first thing for one to do in making ready for the duties of citizenship is to be sure that he has a sufficient understanding as to what his people have been striving for before his time, not only what they have deliberately been endeavouring to do, but, what is more important, the direction which has been given to their actions, by them unplanned, through the beneficent rule which controls the world.

To gain a basis for the fuller understanding of the patriot's task the student should acquaint himself

SHARE OF THE AVERAGE MAN 51

with the history of his people. This should extend at least as far back as the beginnings of English history, and may well include something of the story of the Jews, the Greeks, and the Romans of antiquity, and of the French, the Germans, the Spaniards, and Swiss of modern times. English history is, to the American, of first importance for the reason that our speech, laws, modes of life, and ways of thinking on political matters have come to us from Great Britain, and have not been greatly changed in their transfer from the old world to the new. The Spanish and French histories are important as they show us many instructive contrasts with our own, and also for the reason that those nations shared largely in the settlement of the Americas, and have left their mark on many parts of our country. The history of Switzerland is of value for the reason that it is the one European state which has attained to a federal republican government essentially like our own, modelled, indeed, upon it, and which is in certain important ways more successful than that of our United States.

The study of American history should begin with reading, which will give a clear knowledge of the natural features of the country, — its climate, products of the soil, and under-earth and other conditions which determine the fitness of the land and of its several parts for the uses of man. If this reading is done with the use of good maps, the student may gain a tolerably clear notion as to the characteristics of the portion of the continent which has fallen to the lot of his folk. The study will not only show him the stage on which the people have played their part, but it will enable him to understand the diversities of their qualities so far as these diversities depend on the character of the world about them.

On the above-noted foundation the history of our people may be set. The study of this should begin with the work of the explorers who first revealed the wonders of the land to our race. There the French have the first place. Their labours and adventures are admirably told by the historian Parkman. The French, as the record will show, were as eminent as pathfinders of the wilderness as they have been unsuccessful in winning it to their empire. It is well worth while to note that they at one time held, by the right of discovery and of some slight efforts at settlement, the greater part of the Mississippi valley, while the next important river basin, that of the St. Lawrence, as well as the lands about the gulf of that name, were theirs for more than a century; yet this promising empire of the early days of the colonies faded away before the strength of the English people, and has left no trace except it be in the presence of the French-speaking people of Canada, and many names in the countries from which they have vanished. St. Louis, Vincennes, Des Moines, as well as the appellations of a host of streams and lakes, recall the part France once had in our country, as other names do that of the banished Indians, with a startling suggestiveness of the incapacity of certain peoples to hold their place in the struggle for existence.

The student may well consider the reason for this failure of the French, who were so daringly successful in exploring and planting colonies in the wilderness of America, to make good their claim to the land. He will find the answer in the fact that our English people, where they settle in a new country, do not found colonies in the common sense of the word, but rather sow the seed of states which depend for their nurture not on the sustenance of the mother country, but on their own strength. It is this quality of those of our race and speech which has lined the shores of the seas with their establishments giving them dominion of the fairest parts of the earth; assuring them dominance of it so long as they hold to the kinship of race and purpose which should knit them firmly together.

The colonial history of this country needs to be understood, at least as regards its outlines, in order to see how the original diversities of population and motive became, by the state-making ability of our English people, converted into a true nation having a more really united character than has ever been given to any like numbers of folk. Interesting and instructive as is the story of our revolutionary period and of the development which has come about since that time, including the vast struggle of the Civil War, that of the earlier days has even more to tell the student of liberty, for there he may see the first and shaping stages of its American development. On the sturdy independent motive of the Puritan English of the mother country, as shown in Hampden and his fellows, he may see arising the larger feeling as to the position of men which in the end found its expression in the phrase that rings the world round, — "All men are born free and of equal rights."

Every young American should learn the steps by which the colonies worked their difficult way to an effective union of the originally distinct settlements. In most American histories the writers have given much attention to the Revolutionary War, as if that were the principal matter of the struggle to found this nation. Interesting as were the military incidents of the Revolution, they differed in no important respects from those of many another conflict. More brilliant campaigns, more heroic endurance of trials, greater sacrifices in the cause of country, can be found in the records of other states and times. The really admirable part of the story begins when the patriots, having won their independence after some years of war, came to the task of uniting the several colonies so that a nation should arise where before there were

SHARE OF THE AVERAGE MAN

separate and contending states, the people of which had in their earlier days been much given to disputes with one another. Then began a memorable and truly American work, one in which we may justly take great pride, for the like of it was never before done. From their failure to meet successfully just such needs as the founders of our republic dealt with, Greece fell before the power of Rome, and many a modern country, such as Germany, Holland, and Italy, long remained the prey of foreign invaders.

To know how our federal Constitution came to exist is to understand the ideals of our government. The whole scheme of that contract is singularly original; it came from men who had learned principles of liberty; particularly, that political freedom involves a recognition of the rights of men and demands a very clear and unalterable definition of those rights. It is most important that the student should trace the debates that led to the adoption of the Constitution, for they show him how the shapers of our government laboured to frame that masterly piece of statecraft.

The history of this country after the adoption of the federal Constitution is principally interesting and important to those who are preparing themselves for the duties of citizenship from two points of view. The first of these concerns the foreign policy of the country, the second the relation between the states and the federal government, and as an incident to this the long, and in the end fatal, debate concerning the institution of slavery. On these two great questions every American citizen should be informed, for on them has depended the greater features in the history of his country.

The foreign policy of this country was determined not by any terms of the Constitution or any laws, but by the common consent of the very able and patriotic men who guided our affairs in the time when the principles of our government were being formed. These statesmen knew the effects to be expected from a mingling of this country in the contests between great states of the world for colonial possessions which lead to war as their usual, indeed, we may say necessary, result. Thus, when in his farewell address at the close of his second term as president Washington advised his countrymen to beware of entangling alliances with foreign powers, he expressed the convictions of the leaders of his time. In the term of his successor in the presidency there came a singular test as to the willingness of our people to follow the advice of their great leader in the matter of foreign relations. During our Revolution France, as the price of the help she gave the revolting colonies, required them to agree to take up arms against Great Britain on any occasion when she should be at war with that country. The condition was preposterous, yet it was accepted by our people in the way in which men in dire need will agree to terms

SHARE OF THE AVERAGE MAN 57

that they cannot morally make binding on those that are to come after them. When the demand came that we — then at peace with the mother country — should attack her, the authorities of the United States refused to keep the contract. The whole matter was very humiliating, but it was useful, as it served to fix the determination of the people not to enter into the politics and wars of the states on the other side of the sea. Thus they avoided among other ill chances the dangers which are brought about by great standing armies.

Having determined on a policy of peace with its sister nations, our country has adhered to it in a tolerably consistent way, having engaged in wars with foreign peoples only thrice in more than a century. More than once it has had to chastise the barbarians of distant parts of the world, as in the case of the Algerian pirates who preyed upon our commerce as they had done with impunity on that of the European states for centuries. We have likewise had many little creditable though inevitable conflicts with our American Indians, who naturally resented the western movement of our people. Only in one case, that of the Mexican War, have we deliberately entered on the paths of military conquest. In this affair we won much territory, including California, but for all that we lost in honour. The incident was as discreditable to the nation as all such preying of stronger states on the weaker is sure to be, and the profit from it in accessions of territory cannot redeem our action.

The main debate concerning the relations between the federal government and the several states as to the measure of the powers belonging, under the Constitution, to the one and the other, began with the framing of the federal Constitution. The separate colonies disliked to give up their independence to a government which was not yet definitely in existence, to which they could not feel much patriotic allegiance, and from which they feared some kind of tyranny. Therefore it was necessary to leave this matter as to the sharing of powers in a rather indefinite form; a somewhat ill-defined union of the colonies seemed then and perhaps was in fact better than none at all. Time, however, showed the inevitable danger of making contracts where the conditions of the most important part of the matters are left unstated. From the year the Constitution was ratified by the several states until 1861, there was an unending strife as to the right of the federal government to compel a state to obey any of the acts of Congress, a large party holding that a state could refuse to accept or nullify any such act at its pleasure.

If the United States had been a really united body of people, it is likely that the question of state rights would have been settled by the common consent as to the advantages of a strong federal authority. But the institution of African slavery, which originally existed throughout the country, had become practically limited to the so-called southern states, divided the people in habits of life and thought, as well as in business interests, into two naturally hostile camps. Those of the slaveholding states saw clearly that their system of labour was threatened by the more rapid growth of the free commonwealths of the north, and that the rising sentiment against slavery would in time lead to an overthrow of the institution by some form of federal action. Thus the states' rights question, in itself a matter of grave moment, one that needed much consideration, became entangled with the fate of an institution which from the beginning was seen by all right-minded people to be a curse to the country, one which had eventually to be cleared away.

The debates concerning the unhappily mixed question of states' rights and slavery constitute what is perhaps the most interesting chapter in the history of the nineteenth century. It is well that every citizen should be familiar with them, for in no other way will he so readily come to understand the quality of his people, or see how the spirit of the mass of its citizens expresses itself in deeds. We will see how the contest against slavery, beginning with a few plain people outside of politics, mostly Quakers, gradually appealed to the body of the citizens of the non-slaveholding states, who were in general determined that the area of slavery should not be extended, and that so far as might be it should be put in the way of extinction. In no other country has a moral purpose been so effectively accomplished.

The armed resistance of the greater number of the slaveholding states after their effort to separate from the Union, ending in the overthrow of the revolutionists, showed the capacity of our folk to meet grave internal troubles in a vigorous way; still more, it indicated the willingness of the people of the whole country, Northerners and Southerners alike, to pay with their lives for their convictions as to principles of government. The men of both sides were animated by patriotic convictions as to their duty by their commonwealths. As far as war can be so, the struggle was honourable alike to victor and vanquished. The student may, if he please, acquaint himself with the history of the campaigns of the Civil War, but except he desires to study the matter from the point of view of military science, a very difficult branch of learning, or to obtain an idea of the valour of his people, they will not repay him for his trouble; the time and labour had much better be given to the political history of the period which contains a great deal that every American needs to know.[1]

---

[1] I am glad to see reasons for believing that our people are very properly neglecting the military history of the Civil War. I recently asked, in succession, one hundred intelligent young people, all of whom might reasonably be supposed to have a fair knowledge of the history of their country, for information concerning the battle of Perryville or

The most interesting result of the Civil War, next after the extinction of slavery and of the doctrine of nullification, is to be found in the fact that the essential principle of states' rights came forth from the conflict unchanged, the states being left with their old and fit share of power with their partial independence as states. In no other instance has a conflict such as that of our Civil War so little harmed or even changed the institutions of a country. In most cases such struggles result in great alterations in the nature of the government and the rights of the people. It is an admirable proof of the sagacity and statesmanship of the founders of our nation that the storms of war left the structure which they built uninjured. The only evident permanent effects of the trial was to free the slaves and to give an opportunity for new life to the southern states, which had been sorely hampered by the evils of the slaveholding system.

American history is so complicated and so full of details that few citizens can afford the time to become familiar with it; but if the student will make himself acquainted with the work done in forming

Chaplin Fork. No one of them had ever heard of the place, yet it was the scene of a remarkable conflict, one in which about eight thousand men were put out of the fight in less than two hours, and where the conditions of the action were, from a military point of view, most extraordinary. The slaughter was so swift that more men were killed and wounded in a like short time and with like numbers than in any other battle in modern days. The loss was about as great as it was during the whole Revolutionary War.

the Federal Union, with the attitude of our nation towards foreign countries, and with the history of the slavery conflict, including the matter of states' rights, he will have sufficient clues to the course of our national affairs. It may be well also for him to trace the history of the money problems in this country, and the dealing of our government with the Indians, whom we were forced to drive out of their lands in order to win room for our increasing population. Neither of these records is pleasant reading to an American, for they both abound in follies and disgraces. The first of these unhappy experiences is over; the Indians have been forced upon the lands which are allotted for their occupation and compelled to keep the peace; the long conflict with them is at an end. The second question, that which relates to money, is now that which most exercises our people. Unfortunately, it is, of all the problems which a government has to face, the most difficult; the trouble with us is that it has to be dealt with by a popular vote, while it needs the judgment of the best-trained financiers, of men who are experts in the matter, for its proper ordering.

As the student follows the history of this country he will do well to note the fact that in all matters relating to the liberty of the individual and to the development of his powers by education, great success has been attained, — a success which is far more distinguished than that which has been won in

SHARE OF THE AVERAGE MAN 63

any other country except, it may be, in Switzerland, where the development of free institutions and of free men has been going on for a much longer time than with us, and where the results are fairly comparable with our own. The failures with us have been mostly in matters which, though important, such as the economy of our government, the appointment of officers, and the management of the political parties, are less essential than those which relate to the intelligent freedom of the citizen. Given true national liberty with its attendant love of right doing and keen sympathy with the needs of the fellow-man, we may be sure that the way to better these ills will be found.

From this glance at the main course of our government — it should be understood that it is rich — we shall now turn to the second part of the subject of this book, wherein we may consider the practical conduct of the citizen in his every-day relations with his fellow-men, which relate to public affairs. The examples of duty which we shall have to consider will often lead us back to the history of land and people; few things in politics or statecraft, or, for that matter, in any field of action, can be understood without knowing how they came to be as we find them.

CHAPTER V

THE PRACTICE OF CITIZENSHIP

THE true value of all a man may know or think concerning the rights and duties of the citizen consists in the application he may make of his knowledge and thought to the work of the state in which he dwells. It is not too much to say that even as a man cannot become an athlete by meditating on gymnastics, so he cannot become an effective patriot by the mere accumulation of information concerning public affairs, or of his good-will towards his fellow-men. To attain any valuable result, the man must persistently *act* for the good of his people. There is a common and very harmful notion that in order to do public service a man must hold some public office. The truth is that the best work of this nation, that which controls the quality of its people, is done in their households, in their local associations, relating to churches, etc., and in the lowest — should we not rather say highest — stages of governmental work, that of precincts or towns. In these fields of activity the spirit of the freeman is made; if the making is there well done, that which comes from the legislatures may

PRACTICE OF CITIZENSHIP 65

be trusted to have a like quality; if the local life be not of a high citizenly character, all the constitutions and congresses in the world will not give the people true freedom.

To get an idea as to the value of local life of a people in relation to liberty, the reader will do well to look into the condition of the so-called republics of Central and South America, — states which, in their constitutions and their laws, are almost exactly like our own. They too were revolting colonies which, on attaining their independence of Spain, adopted the system of the government which originated in the United States, with the idea that the likeness of constitutions would give them the same good result that had been won with us. Not having the spirit of true liberty which makes free states, these Spanish-American countries have never become true republics. They are governed by a ruling military class, the masses of the people having no effective share in the control of the state. The elections are to a great extent mere shams. The presidents are usually despots. The power which is not in the hands of the usurping tyrant is in that of men who form an oligarchy, or, in other words, a governing aristocracy, the members of which do not come to their place by inheritance, but because they have gained wealth or station. These countries are now merely pretending to be democracised; it may be that in time they will through education create the freeman who may make their constitutions and laws have real meaning; at present they show that the men of a republic must exist before a state of that quality can be made.

As the basis of his understanding of local government the student should consider the household. That, as has been noted, is the necessary basis of government; it has ever been the cradle of all the qualities which make for high citizenship, — the primary school where the youth acquired the essentials of thought and action. In the home the youth learns, if he is ever to acquire it, the habit of kindly and free understanding with those about him, on which all true citizenship rests. He then learns the great lessons of obedience to superior wisdom, to the authority of those who have to be masters because it is for the time their duty to manage the little state beneath the family roof. The consideration one for another; the daily reward of mutual labour; the subjection of individual desires to the common good, — are lessons of the home which are to be applied to the work of the larger commonwealth. Therefore the first care of the citizen, a truly statesmanly care, is by the household of which he forms a part. We may well take note of the important truth that in all structures of any kind there is some unit which is the basis of its existence. Thus in all matter we have the enduring atom with its unchanging characters; in every animated body its cells; in

PRACTICE OF CITIZENSHIP 67

our frames, as in all the higher animals, these cells are combined into organs, which by their qualities afford the higher life.

In the structure of the state the household or home is the unit of development. So long as it is strongly united by the ties of affection and inspired with the motives of duty, education, and religion, the society which rests upon it is secure. Thus in the case of the southern states which were brought to utter political and financial ruin at the end of our Civil War, — a ruin more disastrous than that which has overtaken any civilised country in modern times, for the reason that it involved the complete overthrow of the labour system of the region, — the quick recovery of the people from the appalling disaster was due to the fact that the households were of a high type and were unbroken by the shock. They were ready to send forth young men and women fit to meet the trials of the new life of labour and self-dependence. Owing to this goodness of the homes in the ruined confederacy, a quality which they shared with the other parts of this country, and owing to the blessed fact that the home is the most indestructible of all the institutions of men, this unhappy portion of our land in greater part recovered from its losses within twenty years after the end of the war. It may fairly be said that any country of which the homes are strong enough to make it suited for a democratic government could survive the destruction of all its institutions and all its property beyond the walls of the households, with the certainty that the people would quickly restore their losses.

Therefore it may not be said too strongly that the first duty of the citizen is by the home which brought him up to his station; his care should be to preserve and strengthen it in every way he can. Whether he be the head of the household in which he dwells, or only a subordinate member of it, he should regard his life therein as a continued and effective opportunity to support the commonwealth. In the field of larger politics the most sincere and arduous endeavours are likely enough to result in failure, but in the household every worthy effort bears fruit in the enlarged quality of its members and their increased fitness for the duties of the citizen. This field of the home is not only the most profitable for patriotic labour, but it is by far the easiest in which to win good results, for the gain depends on simple and easily attainable things, on sympathetic helpfulness, forethought for others, and in care for their instruction.

Next above the household, in order not of value but of magnitude, comes a larger governmental unit which, in different parts of this country, varies much in name and nature. In New England it is the town with its admirable government by parliaments of the voters, and by their delegates, the selectmen.

PRACTICE OF CITIZENSHIP 69

In other country parts of the United States it is the town, precinct, parish, hundred, or school district; where these divisions are lacking or of no account, the lowest stage of formal government is the county. In all these governmental arrangements which are nearest to the people the aim of the machinery is to perform those services which are of immediate importance to their ordinary needs, — the care of schools and libraries, of roads and bridges, of paupers, the police, public halls, burial places, etc. It should include matters relating to health, water supply, and the ornamentation, or at least the prevention, of defacement of the locality.

Only where the New England town system exists do we find the local governments of this country in its best shape to do the work which falls to them. In that system the voters, assembled in town meeting, debate all the projects which are brought before them for consideration. Of these one is commonly held each year to determine the general policy of the town, and for voting taxes, as well as for the election (in some states) of town officers. Others to deal with emergencies may be held on the demand of a certain number of the citizens. This system is admirable in many ways: in the first place, for the reason that it is a government by the parliamentary method, or, as the word means, by a free discussion of things proposed to be done; in the second place, it gives every voter a chance to take an intelligent share in the control of public affairs, not by the choice of representatives, but by his own direct action.

So long as the towns are small, having, say, not more than five hundred voters, the New England system is by far the best method of local government that has ever been contrived; it combines the advantages of directness and publicity in the management of the interests of the people with a training of the citizens in legislation which is of very great value to them. Unfortunately this institution is limited to a small part of this country, the greater portion having the local governments so organised that the people merely elect their masters, such as those having charge of the schools, commissioners who have to do with roads, etc., or the officers charged with town government, such as the councilmen or aldermen, leaving to them the decision of all matters, and with no other control or immediate criticism of their actions than what is given by the power to put in new men at the next election. It is very much to be desired that the town parliament method should be extended throughout this country. In the greater number of our states it will require no considerable attention in the constitutions to bring this change about. We may, perhaps, look to some patriotic young man who reads these words to be the leader in this important reform in the method of local government, which is so necessary in all parts of this country which lie to the west and south of the Hudson River.

As before remarked, a democracy founded on well-conditioned homes can be made to work with almost any kind of governmental machinery, but that which has been provided for it in American communities where the town of the New England type does not exist is about the worst that could be contrived. It is the survival of the English parish system, in which a few important men selected by birth, by appointment, or by the choice of the church members, were given authority in such measure that the common people of the locality had little to do with their own affairs. Until a reform can be brought about which will perhaps be difficult to accomplish, there is nothing to do but to make the existing conditions give the best possible results.

In the cities of this country the methods of local government are even more defective than in the rural districts. In these large towns the numbers of people are so great and they know so little of one another that it is almost impossible to obtain anything like a democratic government such as depends upon the sympathy and mutual understanding of the citizens. This difficulty in the management of our cities calls for all the skill of our patriotic men in order to keep the people who are crowded into them from losing all the qualities of true freemen.

The statements which have just been made concerning the conditions of our local governments apply with even more force to those of the next higher stage in the machinery, — that which has control of the counties. In the counties of the United States we have a curious survival, in name and nature, of an English system which dates from feudal times, when the lands were partitioned among chieftains. These men ruled much as independent sovereigns, owing only a certain limited allegiance to their king. When this system was broken up, the crown appointed a lord-lieutenant to be the head man for each of these ancient dominions, which still remained separated from each other in many important ways. When, in the time of Elizabeth and of her immediate successors, the beginnings of the American colonies were made, there was the influence of old customs to lead men to make the main divisions of their states by counties, and to adopt, so far as might be, the method of governing them which existed in the mother country.

Very naturally the American county came to have its officers elected by the people. The court-house in the shire town, with its place of public records, its county court offices, its commissioners charged with the care of public property, were elected; but as the counties were generally large and the matters in the hands of its officers not easily to be scrutinised by the people because they were remote from the seat of government, and especially as there is little or no

PRACTICE OF CITIZENSHIP 73

opportunity for public debate concerning the administration, this part of our local government by counties has not proved successful, and may well be termed a failure. Where the town system exists, as in the northeastern states, and the county authorities have little to do except with such matters as courts and records, and the charge of the main roads and the public buildings, this method of government is not so distinctly bad; but when the local affairs, save it may be the district schools, are managed from the shire town, the system often leads to inefficiency and to the neglect of local needs, evils from which the county governments in this country very generally suffer.

In undertaking to do his fit share in that part of his government which is next his hand, the citizen should make himself familiar with the ways in which its work is done. If he has been so fortunate as to have been born in a region where the parliamentary town system exists, he is likely to have made the acquaintance of that method, at least so far as the annual meeting goes, for the boys usually have a chance to hear the debates. If, as is most likely, his lot has been cast in a part of the country where the local government is not thus carried on, he will have to learn the way the machine works at second hand, by watching how the business is regulated by the officers elected to care for it.

As soon as the citizen is of age to have a vote, he

should at once begin to take his share, not alone as an observer, but as an active member of the body of voters. To do his duty by this task, as by any other, he should proceed to study the ways in which he can make his work count in the most effective manner. Here comes in the element of judgment in public affairs which all need to acquire, and which may best be gained in action. It is not easy to advise in this matter, but there are certain indications of value which may be given.

In any community it is easy for any educated, patriotic citizen to see certain evils which should be remedied. It may be a road that is in such condition that it is a burden on the farmers and to others who have to use it; a school that is not doing the work it should, or perhaps some "ring" or set of people who are mismanaging the public affairs. There is no better task for a young man who would begin his citizenly duty than for him to set about the reform of the first evil in public affairs that it may seem in his power to remedy. In no other manner will he so quickly learn something of public business, and especially of the difficulties which beset the efforts of the reformer. He is likely enough to fail in his first efforts, but the history of government shows full well that any earnest, patriotic man may hope so to impress his fellow-citizens that they will follow his lead, provided he makes the path of duty plain to them.

Where the citizen essays reforms he will find that the chance of success depends upon his ability to convince a number of his fellows that the cause he has espoused is just, and that it is their duty to devote themselves to that cause; he must in a sense form a party. We shall have to consider in a somewhat detailed way the relation of the citizen to parties in the common meaning of the word; it need only be said here that all democratic action in the way of reform or betterment has to be brought about by the creation of temporary parties; that is, associations of persons who work together for a common end. In fact, the first and most admirable task of the patriot is to learn the art of persuading his neighbours to join him in making improvements in the affairs of his neighbourhood. He not only accomplishes the particular betterment, but he trains himself and his associates in the best of political art. There is no place in this country which does not afford ample opportunities for the exercise of patriotic duty in such work. It is well to remember that any democratic society that is not improving is sure to be going backwards. It is only where the people are constantly exercised in reforming their society that they have a chance to develop the qualities of patriotism that serve to keep it alive.

The opportunities of the citizen in relation to the government of his state, and to the nation of which the state forms a part, are more limited than are those which come to him from the locality in which he dwells. In local affairs he sees the needs with his own eyes, and may act in a direct way; in the matters relating to the wider field he has to judge by hearsay and to act with such a number of people that his personal influence is less than he might hope for in local affairs. Fortunately the questions which come before the state and national governments, though important, are less vitally so than are those which concern the towns, cities, or other parts of the political machinery which are in immediate contact with the people. It is in general true that the nearer the government to the man, the more it may affect his honour, his property, or the other conditions of his life. Therefore, while the state and federal governments suffer most from a lack of scrutiny by the people who maintain them, the evils which thus arise are usually less important than they would be if they befell the local parts of the system.

In the states of this country the principal duty of the state government is to maintain the system of the courts, to care for the prisons and asylums, and to have general charge of the corporations which do business within its limits, such as the railways, manufacturing companies, etc. The states have also more or less to do with the public-school system, taking general charge of this part of the educational machinery. In some states their governments undertake public improvements, such as building main roads; where the territory borders on the sea or the Great Lakes the authorities have charge of such harbours as are not, because of their importance in relation to foreign commerce, in the control of the federal authority; so, too, in matters relating to public health, the states have of late years generally come to exercise a certain amount of control, in order to suppress plagues among cattle and epidemics among men; for this reason they may have authority over the sources of water supply, and allot them to the localities where they are needed. Experience shows a prevailing tendency in this country for the states gradually to do more and more of the work which originally belonged to the local governments, that is, the towns and counties. In the main, this change has proved beneficial, yet it has the danger that the work thus done is kept out of the sight and mind of the people who pay for it and who should care for it.

The only way to meet the danger which is incurred from having a large part of the work of a government done at a distance from the people is by exercising a peculiar care as to the character and ability of the men who are chosen to represent the people; this care is very necessary as regards all those to whom authority is delegated, but it is peculiarly so in those cases where the work is done as it is in our state and federal legislatures, under conditions which make it wellnigh impossible for the private citizens to have any real knowledge of what laws are made, and how they are likely to affect the people.

The difficulty which exists in a citizenly oversight of the state governments is even greater in the matter of federal legislation, for the Congress of the United States is very remote from the people. The members of the Senate are not chosen by direct vote, but by the state legislators, each for a term of six years. It is therefore not to be expected that these senators will be known at all by any considerable number of the people. The members of the lower federal house represent on an average about two hundred thousand citizens. They are about as little known to their constituents in a personal way as the members of the Senate. This is to be regretted, for the condition of an ideal or even a sound democracy is a close, sympathetic understanding between the plain citizen and the man he chooses to care for his interests in places of authority. These evils are in the nature of things; in a small country it is possible to hold to the early, simple ways in which each citizen might know the man to whom he intrusted his rights, his property, and his share of the national good repute; with our people, ever increasing in numbers, we have constantly to trust more and more to such imperfect control as we may be able to keep over the members to the state and national legislatures, by turning out

PRACTICE OF CITIZENSHIP

men who do wrong rather than by putting in men who we know will do right.

The most effective control over the conduct of legislators is to be found in the generally patriotic motive of American citizens. With comparatively few exceptions, the men who have the ability which enables them to attain such stations are naturally desirous of doing faithful service. Except when self-interest prompts them overmuch, or when they have become mere servants of a party, they are likely to do their duty according to their light. Although our partisan newspapers are much given to denouncing the representatives who belong to the party they oppose, it is the opinion of those who are in a position to form a fair judgment in the matter that these men are usually trustworthy, and that their errors are with rare exceptions due to excessive party spirit, or to an inability to comprehend large matters of government. Nevertheless, it is evident that our federal Congress and the state legislatures are not always competent to deal with the questions which are presented to them. These questions are in this day much more varied in their nature and more complicated than they were in the days of our fathers. The trouble seems to lie in the fact that in our time the ablest men no longer are willing to devote themselves to politics; they prefer the successes of business or professional life to the turmoil of elections and the abuse which every man who enters politics may expect to encounter, however faithful he may be to his trust.

Each citizen has a chance to take a part in the nomination of candidates for most offices through the primary elections or the caucuses. When he comes to his share in this work he is likely to find that the machinery of the meetings is in the hands of some clique who, because of the negligence of the mass of the voters, has, though it is usually a small minority of the whole party, gained the power to nominate their men. In some cases this so-called "ring" owes its existence merely to the fact that the people who compose it have an active interest in political affairs; that they regularly attend the caucuses, and so, because of the lack of care of the majority of their political belief, have the power to "run the party." It sometimes happens that these people make a business of managing the elections for their own profit. Until very recent years it was possible for the ruling men in each party to reward those who were diligent in its work by a great variety of gifts in the way of offices which are well paid. This has been to a great extent changed by the extension of the civil-service system to nearly all the offices which have hitherto been the rewards that politicians have bestowed upon their followers. Hereafter we may reckon that the patriot citizen will find less difficulty in organising his fellows of the better sort to control the nominations of his party.

PRACTICE OF CITIZENSHIP

The success of representation which has to be the foundation of any but the local government of a democracy depends upon the skill of the electors in choosing the right kind of men for the duties which are to be imposed upon them. It is evident that this choice should fall not upon men who for lack of other employment are hungry for the place, but upon those who have proved their ability to achieve success in life in other ways than public service, and who take office as a duty, and not because they need it, — persons who have succeeded in business of the true sort, not in speculation, such as the better class of lawyers, and other proficient men, intelligent farmers, and sometimes schoolmasters. It would seem that men of inherited fortune, education, and capacity should prove in this country, as they have in England, valuable helpers to their fellow-citizens in the tasks of government, but for some reason, with rare though admirable exceptions, this has not proved to be the case; with us such men do not appear to have the business training which is even more required of the American legislator than of those who sit in the parliaments of the old world.

In general it may be said that no man is fit to be trusted with the care of the interests of the people who does not live in an honourable manner. He should be a man of family and of good repute; he should be known as trustworthy in money matters. If he has managed public affairs in any position, his record there should be scanned, for it may be assumed that his quality will remain the same in whatever station he occupies. There are few rules without exceptions, and so instances could be cited from our own public men where persons of bad moral character have been useful officers of the state, but these exceptions are so rare that they may safely be neglected. Statecraft is like any other serious business, in which the employer would show himself a fool who trusted his affairs to a dissolute or scampish fellow because he had ability.

There is a common notion that the legislator should be an orator. Than this there is no greater error as to the capacities needed by such men. There was a time when brilliancy in debate was an element of strength in a legislator, when he could win votes for his cause by that means, but that stage of our public life has passed away. A Webster or a Clay at his best could not be expected in this day greatly to influence the action of a legislature. A capacity to state matters clearly, so that intelligent action on them may be obtained is necessary, but this may be reckoned on in any man of good ability.

When an able and honest legislator or other public officer has been chosen for a place of important responsibility, he thereby becomes entitled to the support and confidence of all the people he represents. Though elected by one party, his duty is by the whole community, and it is the duty of that community to support him. He therefore should, while in office, be upheld by every citizen of every party, whether they voted for him or no. This course is not only just and patriotic, but it is from motives of expediency in a high degree important. No public officer can be expected to escape the evils of a partisan state of mind who feels that all his fellow-citizens except those who gave him their votes are his enemies. Often so bitter is this hatred that his political opponents will without good cause and from mere brutal ill-nature defame him in any way they can. Such a disgraceful course tends to degrade our politics more than any other influences with which we have to contend.

When an able man has served his people well in any place of responsibility, it is the best policy to keep him in the position as long as he is willing to fill it. In grave political crises it may be the duty of the citizen to remove a serviceable legislator in order that some important measure may be sure of a majority, but such changes are always to be regretted, and should be made only where necessary to accomplish large purposes. It is often better to retain a trustworthy and effective man who differs from us on certain points of policy than to risk the chance of finding some other whose belief is nearer to our own, but whose general capacity as a servant of the state may be of a much lower grade. Here we find ourselves in face of the most troublesome questions that the young citizen has to consider, that is, that of parties and party allegiance; it will therefore be well to turn at once to the consideration of this matter.

CHAPTER VI

CITIZENSHIP AND PARTY ALLEGIANCE

WE have already noted the fact that when a man endeavours to accomplish any public action for the benefit of his neighbourhood he has to begin the work by finding other men who can be brought to a like mind, and who are willing to combine with him in a common effort to have the thing done; in other words, he has to form a party. Each year, then, are thousands of these temporary political organisations formed and dissolved in different parts of the country, each having accomplished its purpose, or having so clearly failed to do so that the people who were interested in the particular matter have lost courage to continue their efforts. It not infrequently happens that the particular end which is sought, — as, for instance, the construction of some important work, such as the Erie Canal, — takes many years, so that the temporary party endures for the lifetime of a generation. Now and then it happens that the evil which a party aims to remedy — as, for instance, the institution of African slavery or the enslaving of the government clerks by the politicians — requires a long time for its abolition, so that the party has to keep up its work for a half-century or more. In a good democratic soil the growth of parties is as incessant as that of vegetation from the earth: some die in a season after having borne more or less good seed; others are century plants; yet others may endure, like great oaks, for thousands of years.

When the aim of a party is to bring about some moral change in the conditions of the people, such as the suppression of drunkenness or other vice, because of the difficulty of improving the conduct of men, the association is sure of a long life; only in a few cases has it happened that it dissolves because its work is completely done. The most notable instance of this was in the case of the antislavery party, which passed away because its task had been accomplished in all parts of the civilised world.

There is yet another group of parties, the longest-lived and most characteristic of such organisations, which relate to the views of the citizens concerning the principles on which the states or the nation shall be governed. Those of the lesser sort which concern immediate needs are common among all peoples which have any measure of freedom or the advancement which goes therewith. The larger truly political parties only take on their most perfect form in really free countries, — such as the United States, England, or Switzerland. In the United States the people are by nature or by early training generally divided into two groups, which, though in earlier times they were otherwise named, are at present known with us as Democrats and Republicans. The former was originally termed Republicans, or Republican Democrats; the latter has borne in succession the title of Federalist, Whig, and finally that of Republican. In England similar parties have long existed under other names; the equivalent of our Democratic organisation has been called Whig, and is now known as Liberal; that somewhat corresponding to our Republican party was once the Tory and is now Conservative. Similar divisions are traceable in other European countries; the nearer the states of that region approach to freedom, the more distinctly do these two parties appear, and the larger their share in the national life.

Looked at from a non-partisan point of view, the two great parties of a free state are seen to represent two diverse theories of government. The one which is represented by our existing Republican organisation holds to the idea of a strong central power in the nation which, while fully representing the people, shall strengthen the government so that it can in many ways send its influence down to every part of the country and abroad throughout the world. It favours legislation that may by tariffs or taxes on foreign products lead to the development of internal manufacturing, so that the people shall, so far as may be, make all the goods which they consume. It seeks to increase the power of the central or federal government, if needs be, at the cost of that which the separate states may hold; in other words, it starts with the ideal of the consolidated nation rather than with that of an aggregation of local governments.

On the other hand, the present Democratic party in general considers as of first importance the government of the locality, be it town, county, or state, and regards the federal government as essentially a means for making these local governments safe from foreign interference or from strife among themselves. It opposes any more control on the part of the central authority than is necessary to accomplish these ends. It is against the establishment of tariffs purely for the sake of protecting internal manufacturing, holding that the people should be allowed to make, buy, and sell in the freest possible manner, guided only by the natural opportunities of their realm. As a result of these views the Democratic party is, at least in theory, opposed to having the federal government take much share in foreign affairs.

To the general projects of the two great parties as above outlined, there are, from time to time, with the changing drift of public opinion, added a great variety of temporary purposes and projects relating to currency, taxes, internal improvements, the authority of the courts, etc. In fact, these incidental growths are so numerous, and from time to time so

PARTY ALLEGIANCE

important, that they are likely to overshadow the main issues of the parties. Many will therefore question the accuracy of the descriptions which have been given of them; but those who have studied the history of these organisations are likely to agree with the writer that they rest in two natural divisions in the ways in which men look upon government: some looking to the superior state and others to the neighbourhood; some valuing most highly the rights and freedom of the individual man, next that of the local governments, and lastly that of the nation; others giving first value to strong central authority, able to control the whole country and to give the nation strength in its own and other lands.

Both these different views concerning the methods of a free state rest upon noble conceptions of its place and duties in the affairs of men; each has so much to commend it that the patriotic citizen may well be in doubt as to which should command his allegiance. He may indeed have the experience of the writer and many another citizen, and find himself at one time of his life, as during the Civil War, supporting the party of consolidation, — that is, the Republicans, — and again that of local government in the period following that disturbance; in fact, as the changing judgment of our people shows, in the alternations of the elections sometimes one policy appears to them good and sometimes the other. It may often happen that some temporary addition to the projects of a party may lead many men to transfer their support to or from that organisation, as they may object to or approve of the innovations. For all this drifting to and fro, as experience goes to show, the two central parties in the long run are sure to maintain their central ideas; the temporary changes of platforms do not destroy their essential quality. The people need them in their natural shape, and reform them from time to time to meet the requirements of their inborn political desires.

In other countries less free than our own, as in Germany or France, where the people have never had a chance to develop a large measure of liberty, we find that the two normal parties are not, as with us, distinct and permanent, but in their place there are half-a-dozen or more imperfectly divided political sects, each seeking some particular end in legislation, with the result that the state work proceeds without a plan and under conditions of confusion which are dangerous to good government. A national life needs plans for its guidance quite as much as does the life of any of its citizens; the existence of parties which are no better than factions, none strong enough to conduct the government, makes a legislative system very incompetent to do its fit work. Such is the condition now existing in Germany, France, Italy, and generally in Continental Europe. Only in the parliaments of the English-speaking people, because, perhaps, of the essential freedom which those people possess, do we find the plan of two parties usually followed. All the while in these English countries new political organisations are recurrently forming; these in time perish, either because they are merged with the permanent groups, or because, after various trials, the common sense of their adherents tells them that it is not worth while to strive further to win a majority; in other cases these new organisations capture one of the leading parties, or are captured by it, in some of the turns of political manœuvres. So it comes about that though at times there may in this country be more than two strongly supported presidential tickets in the field, such conditions are but temporary; they usually mark a period of unrest which is quickly followed by a reconcentration on the old permanent and natural lines of political campaigns. Thus, in the national election of 1860, just before the Civil War, there were, because of the great division of sentiment, four strong parties in the field, but at the end of that struggle they were again reduced to two. In the presidential campaign of 1896 there were again four such tickets before the country besides that of the Prohibitionists, which perhaps is not to be reckoned in the ordinary sense a political party, but an association of persons who seek a reform in the personal habits of the people.

It is characteristic of the great parties in the

English-speaking countries that they are in a continuous state of growth and change; old issues disappear and new ones take their place. With each of these alterations the quality of the organisation alters for the better or the worse. Sometimes, indeed, we may say very often, a party for a time departs utterly from the path which it should follow; it may indeed stupidly turn back in its track. Such accidents are usually due to the folly of incompetent leaders, who, to gain a temporary advantage, are quite willing to part with their principles; but such accidents are uncommon; they are usually quickly rectified by the action of the honest-minded members of the association, who, from the nature of things, must always constitute the overwhelming majority of any great political body.

That every true political party must be honest-minded may seem an unwarranted statement to many persons who have the unpatriotic habit of regarding their political antagonists as knaves who are endeavouring to ruin the state. A little knowledge of history will show any one that while villains have often been able to form small societies to accomplish their ends, bodies of people have never acted in the party manner except with motives which, though often grievously mistaken, have always rested on sincere beliefs in the righteousness of their cause.

The foregoing sketch of parties will perhaps serve to show that the government of a democracy, because

PARTY ALLEGIANCE

it is a government so well described by Lincoln as "by the people and for the people," must be attained by the party method. It may also show that these associations are but instruments by which the citizen expresses his views as to the policy which he wishes to see adopted in public affairs. If the particular affair be a matter of his locality, he may, as has been suggested, make a party for the purpose of dealing with it. If the question be one of state or national importance, he cannot expect to obtain such an effective following; he can in most instances only give weight to his views, and help his people to attain good ends by acting with one of the existing associations, doing what is in his power to make its purposes good and true. All this serves to prepare our minds for a consideration of the claims that parties have to the allegiance of a man; on their right to hold him to obey the dictates of their caucuses and conventions, by which they determine and carry out their policy.

There can be no question that when a citizen makes it known to any of his fellow-men that he means to act with them in any matter, he thereby becomes honourably pledged to abide with them until the end is attained, or until it becomes clearly evident that it cannot be won by any reasonable sacrifice of time and labour. If he abandons the project, it must be for some other reason than personal interest: an honest change of mind as to the propriety of the undertaking, or as to the trustworthiness of the men who have charge of the task may absolve him from all pledges to the association. Still further, when the party adopts projects which are new and which seem to the voter to be evil, he is morally bound to separate himself from it. In certain cases he may conclude that the leading and original objects of the party are so essential to the good of the country that he must bear with the dangerous novelties in order to make good its safety.

If we look over the history of this or any other democratic country, we see that now one and now another of the two great parties is in possession of the government, but the state remains safe in the hands of either. When the party of consolidation is in power, the drift of affairs is towards the ends they would attain. When that of local government prevails, the opposite drift is noticeable, but the changes are never revolutionary. Therefore, when we clearly see that our party is adopting new and harmful schemes, we should not regard the shouting of the captains concerning our treason, or the ruin of the state which our defection will entail, but spoil their schemes by turning them out of office. Honest men, by voting against their party, thereby putting it in the minority, have a means, often the only one at their command, by which they can clear it of "rings," "bosses," and

PARTY ALLEGIANCE

the other like evils which are likely to infest all long successful political organisations.

It may be easily seen that so long as party managers — men who make politics a business, and sometimes a business of a very low kind — are sure that they can retain the votes and influence of worthy citizens because of their allegiance to the old declared principles of the organisation, they will feel quite safe in their places, whatever they may do; but if they know that these silent men are likely to punish any departure from an honest course by leaving them in a minority, a restraining influence of a very effective kind is placed upon them. Therefore, while the citizen clearly owes an allegiance to the party which represents his ideals of government, he owes it as a freeman, and can in many cases most effectively do his duty, as well as help his party, by refraining to vote for improper candidates, or those who are nominated on platforms which deny the principles of sound government.

We often find that ancient motives are in course of time and change transformed to very different objects from those to which they originally belonged. Thus it is with the spirit of loyalty in public affairs. Of old, men were loyal to their superiors, chiefs, kings, or other aristocratic or military leaders. This devotion was an honourable as well as a necessary thing when the safety of a state in an age of incessant warfare depended on the unquestioned fidelity of the citizens to the commands of those who were intrusted with its safety. In our time there is a tendency to transfer this ancient devotion to parties and to their leaders. Men talk of those who deliberate how they shall vote or who criticise the conduct of their political leaders as if such persons were guilty of treason. Against such vain talk any patriotic citizen should make a firm stand; he may be sure that one of his first duties is to maintain his right to think for himself and to act without fear or favour of any kind. All that is worth having in our state rests on this principle; if any man fails to maintain it, he is guilty of the worst kind of treason, for he assails the very foundations of our government.

It must not be supposed from what has just been said that our political parties are to any great extent or for long left in control of the baser sort of men; assertions to this effect are often made by those who bring to political debate the kind of fury that many men have to work up before they can think or feel in an energetic manner. The managers of these organisations above the lowest grades are usually men of ability and of patriotic motive. They are naturally very eager for success, and, after the manner of men in contests, are apt to go too far in sacrificing principles to immediate profit; they forget that their work is for the state, and that a party, when it ceases to be for the good of the whole

PARTY ALLEGIANCE

commonwealth, should cease to exist. Yet it should be remembered that the evils arising from the leaders turning the influence of political bodies to their private uses is inevitable; it always has to be watched for and punished in a summary way. The fact that the independent voter is subjected to much abuse when he inflicts the punishment may be taken as evidence that the treatment is effective.

One of the most satisfactory features in the present political condition of this country is to be found in the very marked increase in the independence of the voters. So many men of ability and of unquestioned patriotism have of late shown a willingness to chastise their parties by all the means in their power, that in many states there is little influence left to the would-be "bosses;" thus, in time, we may hope for a pretty general uprooting of the evil; already the party whip has ceased to drive men as it did a few years ago.

The great need of our parties in this day is that plain citizens shall study the great questions which are to come before the legislatures; these questions are now too much debated, so far as they are debated at all, by politicians who, from their position as partisans, are led to see but one side of the matter, — a side to which they naturally feel themselves to be pledged. The only safe tribunal is the reason and conscience of the individual voter who considers the problem from the two points of view of the national and personal interests which may be involved therein. It must be acknowledged that the private person is likely to find it difficult to inform himself about the financial or other policies of his government, yet it is by no means impossible for him to do so. The task is a part of the highly educative duty which pertains to his citizenship.

One of the best means for developing a sense of public affairs is to be found in political clubs or debating societies, such as may easily be established in any village where there are half-a-dozen men who may be attracted to the study of statesmanship. If such a club will gather a few books which treat of political economy and the history of American politics; if it will see to it that the different parties have an even chance in the debates, — the result will be most effective. The writer well remembers, when he was a boy of from fifteen to eighteen years of age, how his active membership in such a society enabled him to gain some insight into the great matters of statecraft which were, just before the beginning of the Civil War, agitating the minds of the people. Such political clubs, which existed in great numbers in Kentucky in that period of our history, did much, when the war came, to keep that state from seceding. When the period of debate passed and the time for action came, these clubs naturally ceased to exist; in fact, one of the inevitable evils of the struggle consisted in the general

PARTY ALLEGIANCE

abandonment of debate as means of political education. If a young man is seeking a chance to do some effective work for his neighbourhood, it will be well for him to help in founding a society for political education. It is not necessary, it is, in fact, rather undesirable, that it should be large; it may be effective with but three members; a dozen is ample for the best work.

Next to the debates of the political clubs as agents of education in citizenship, we may set those which in certain parts of the country take place between the leaders of the political parties on the era of a general election. If these contests be carried on by able men, and if they are so arranged that each side has an even share in the debate, the citizen has an opportunity to hear the claims of the two parties; the only difficulty is that the aim of the speakers commonly is, not to attain to the exact truth as the inquirer seeks it, but to win the applause of the mass of his hearers, or, as the ancient phrase has it, to "captivate the vulgar." Such debaters usually have in mind the fact that the greater number of those who hear them do not seek to be convinced by arguments, but rather desire to be pleased by smart sayings or by oratorical flights which flatter their vanity or move their emotions.

It is unhappily true that the great body of the people in any community are not and cannot in the present condition of mankind be expected to attain to any high grade of citizenly accomplishment. They earnestly desire to do the right, but they have neither the ability nor the education to see the way; their course of action must be guided by the leaders of their neighbourhood, — those to whom they have learned to look for the hard thinking which is needed to give sound politics. It should be the aim of every well-trained young man to fit himself to take such a place among his people; if he can help to bring about a condition of affairs where one in a hundred or even one in a thousand of the voters is a man who really knows what the needs of the state are, he will do much to give endurance to the republic. In such conditions the well-meaning but ill-informed body of the people will have a chance of true leadership such as the men who are officially in politics are not likely to afford them.

To be a leader in political thought it is not necessary that a man should be an orator, or that he should be in any way much before the people. As for public speaking, it is most desirable that every educated person should be able to think on his feet before an audience; but his deliverance may well be in a plain-spoken way, for the sole purpose of convincing his neighbours. This is, indeed, the most effective way of presenting truths. In any crisis, great or small, if a citizen feels that he has a thought which may help his fellows, it is his duty, as it should be his pleasure, to state his views, either

PARTY ALLEGIANCE

in public meeting or in print. Our newspapers are usually hospitable in giving any thinking man a chance to say his mind in their pages. If he is able to help them, his fellow-citizens will be glad to read his statements. Much of the most effective influencing of public opinions is thus done by men who seldom or never appear in public meetings.

To sum up this matter concerning the relation of the citizen to political parties, he may say that these institutions are the indispensable agents of a democratic government. Every citizen should foster and respect them; he should regard them as agents which need continual correction, and be prepared to give this by the use of his vote whenever it is clear that punishment for wrong-doing is deserved. It will be well for him to note that each of the great parties is subjected to peculiar dangers. Thus in the Democratic party there is always the risk that the people who desire to break up the social and governmental organisation in the manner of the anarchists, with the vague hope of bettering their condition by the change, may seek to obtain control. There is also a risk that the idea of local government may be carried so far that the central authority may be dangerously weakened. In the Republican party, on the other hand, the chance is that the richer commercial class may manage the state in its interest, increasing the duties on foreign goods to give them a profit in their business, or that they will so enlarge the federal power that the states may not have their fit share in the control of affairs, or that the nation may be led into plans of conquest. Against these defects which occur in either of the great parties, which are indeed the evils which belong with their good qualities, the patriotic citizen has ever to be on his guard. So, too, as regards the conduct of the political managers, he must remember that from their position they are naturally inclined to look rather to party success than to statesmanly accomplishment; they need the quiet criticism of the patriot in private life, who, standing aloof from the thick of the fight, is ready to help, or, if needs be, control the course of action.

CHAPTER VII

ON THE LIMITS OF FREEDOM

BECAUSE the establishment of freedom is a comparatively modern thing, there is, as yet, much doubt and some confusion of mind as to what should be the limits of independent speech and action in a properly regulated democracy. It is easy to set the measure of it in general terms by saying that each shall respect the liberty of all others and not harm the commonwealth in which he dwells; but when we come to determine on the details of action and say that particular things may or may not be done, we find reason for exercising much care. It is, in fact, impossible to set down rules of conduct for all the varying conditions of a society; there are, however, certain limitations which are clear and of universal application.

The first of these rules to which all citizens may fairly be held is that their neighbours shall have the right to think and speak with freedom concerning all public matters. Whatever be their views as to the course of their government or the official conduct of its officers, they have a right to their thought and to its expression in all fit ways. There are certain limitations to this right of expression, but these limitations should themselves be narrowly limited. In all ages men and, through them, their governments have suffered most sorely from restrictions on the freedom of speech. It is, therefore, better to bear with the affliction which comes from hearing opinions we do not share, however preposterous or even disgusting they may seem, rather than to endanger that freedom by any restrictions of law. So far we have lived and, on the whole, prospered under this dispensation. We have for generations allowed all creeds, political as well as religious, to be preached. Even in the Civil War men who held that the secessionists were right were permitted to state their arguments and cast their votes for their convictions. Some really vile beliefs are thus allowed a hearing, but at the same time others, which to the overwhelming majority at first seemed vile, have, through this freedom, in the end won the nation to right ways. This is conspicuously the case with the opposition to slavery.

Of late, with the doubt which many of our people have come to hold as to the safety of our democracy, there has arisen a cry for the limitation of free speech; this has been oftenest heard since the assassination of President McKinley by a man who seems to have been moved to the crime by the public teachings of the anarchists. It has been proposed to pass

THE LIMITS OF FREEDOM

laws that shall make the members of this association criminals, their crime being that they hold the belief that all governments are illegal, and that their rulers should be slain. There could be no better test case on which to try the question as to the right of free speech than this affords. If ever we should set bounds to that freedom, we should do it where men teach murder as a duty. We may, therefore, examine it with care.

It is clear that the anarchists are no common murderers, for they do not slay for gain or for personal revenge. They have the notion that all the most grievous ills from which the masses of men suffer come from a system in which a few rich and strong are able to oppress the many who are poor and weak; that if this ruling class could be deprived of its power the distribution of wealth would be such that all would be prosperous. So far as we have learned, these misguided people are not, except in their main purpose, criminals. They are not thieves, nor do they neglect their children; they are to be reckoned as fanatics, — that is, men with what seems to themselves a moral purpose, but without the sense to see the criminal nature of the means they take to attain it. Practically all of them are foreigners, born under governments of a more or less arbitrary nature, or they are the children of such people who have not become Americanised. In no sense are they the product of this country.

Looking more closely at the cases of assassination of officers of our government, we find but one that can be attributed to this strange political sect. Lincoln was slain by a man who probably had never heard of the anarchists, and who was moved by an insane idea of revenging the overthrow of a cause for which he had not the heart to fight; Garfield by a man who appears to have been crazed by the fierce partisan disputes of his time. So that there has been but one instance in this country where anarchism has been responsible for such a murder, and in this instance the culprit does not appear to have been a member of the association, and his action is denounced by persons who seem to have leadership in it. Therefore the evidence that our commonwealth is in great danger from that evil is not clear.

It may fairly be said that while our institutions do not breed anarchists nor our own people lend themselves to it, other countries have suffered greatly from such fanatics. They have, within a few years, murdered a Russian tsar, an Italian king, an empress of Austria, and a president of the French republic; they have assailed the life of the present King of Great Britain and other chiefs of state; therefore it is urged we should take part in a general effort of all civilised peoples to stamp out the iniquity.

Putting aside the debatable question of whether we are reasonably bound to help countries to sup-

THE LIMITS OF FREEDOM 107

press evils that have grown out of their bad systems of government, let us see what we could do to overthrow the anarchists by any process of law. It is evident that we should have to begin by suppressing all public teaching of doctrines such as these people hold, making it a crime to say that all rulers are the natural enemies of mankind, and as such should be slain. By so doing we might somewhat limit the number of persons who heard of the doctrine, but we should certainly not destroy the sect, as is shown by the experience of Russia, where exile to Siberia, in effect death, awaits all such offenders. The certain result would be to harm the fundamental principle of our political system, — that of free speech. We could go further and make it a penal offence for men to associate themselves, however privately, for the purpose of supporting anarchistic views. By so doing we would drive the members of this sect into hiding, when the only chance of finding them would be by a system of police and spies, such as would be utterly repugnant to our national spirit. How successful this would be we may again judge by the result in Russia, where they do these things much better than we can hope to, yet there are doubtless more and abler anarchists in that country than in any other. In fact, in the Tsar's dominions this sect originated, and there alone it has found support in the educated classes.

Thus, while any effort to suppress the anarchists in this country would be quite certain to fail, the steps we should have to take in order to attain this failure would overthrow the principle that men shall in our commonwealth have the right to think and speak with perfect freedom; that their responsibility to the law is for their deeds alone. If to-day we bid the anarchists be still, we shall have reason to fear that to-morrow some other political sect that holds the germs of good, as that does of evil, may in turn be silenced. It is well to think what would have been the fate of the abolitionists who, a hundred years ago, were, by an overwhelming majority of our people, deemed to be even more dangerous to our state than the anarchists now are.

It has been proposed to exclude the resident anarchists from this country and to prevent immigrants holding that belief from entering it. As for banishing American citizens, or even those of other countries, because of their opinions, it may be said that such a course is at once dangerous and impracticable. Many countries in the past have tried the plan, but none with profit; so that for purposes of punishment or protection it has been disused by most enlightened governments. It has never been used by any English people and is utterly foreign to our ways. If we are to begin it, where is it to end? This is a question ever to be asked when we are called on to limit our ancient liberties. As for

THE LIMITS OF FREEDOM 109

excluding immigrants who may be inclined to anarchism, to what officers of our custom-houses shall be given the supernatural power of discerning the hidden political tendencies of incoming foreigners? While there may be good reasons why we should exclude all ignorant, diseased, or pauper immigrants, or if we please all foreigners who intend to reside in our country, such action should not be taken on account of their opinions. To do so would be to deny the freedom of belief to which we must hold so long as we hope to remain a true democracy.

As for the supposition that assassination of rulers is likely to be a considerable evil in this country, it may be said that while we have grievously suffered in the loss of three men dear to our people, there is no reason to think that any such spirit will ever debase our folk. No one of the three assassins of our Presidents was a characteristic American, in any true measure representing our natures. Except in certain small communities, we find nowhere in this country the cowardly instincts that lead to that form of crime. It thus appears to be better for us to leave this problem with this list of objections to all projects for suppressing the teachings of the anarchists; it is, however, evident that we are not yet, nor are ever likely to be, in the position where we are compelled to pull down the central pillar of our commonwealth in order to save some part of the value of the edifice.

What is evidently needed to make an end of anarchism is first a certain and speedy punishment of all the members of the sect who act on their theories. It may be well with them or with all other assassins to punish their attempts at murder as if they had been successful, for the measure of criminality is not really affected by the results of the culprit's endeavours. It is evident that the deterrent effect of all punishments depends upon the swiftness with which they, by due process of law, follow on the offence for which they are inflicted. In our care for the criminal we have fallen into the bad habit of prolonging the work of the courts, so that when an offender meets his doom his crime is half forgotten; usually the result is that the law, rather than the law-breaker, appears to be on trial. With fit care the process of the courts should be completed with such celerity that even the dull-witted may feel the evident connection of the crime and its penalty. In the tangle of influences which are now leading our people to the evils of mob violence, we must reckon the law's unconscionable delay as not the least, for there is a natural desire to see the murderer, or the assailer of women, brought to swift judgment. There is a rude sense in our common folk that justice to be effective needs follow close on crime.

Next to the swift service of the law, we need a better instruction of ourselves as well as of the

THE LIMITS OF FREEDOM

people we are adopting from other lands in the principles of our government. Our schools are now doing something in the way of formal teaching in the principle of government, but this is as yet not of a nature to awaken in the youth a sense of the meaning of the commonwealth. If he be sensitive to the life about him, he may of himself win to some idea of what our nation is or should be to its citizens; but such teaching is not easy to be had from books; it is of a kind that needs come directly from a teacher. Every school-teacher should know himself or herself to be by position the fittest person to do this great work of awakening youth to a sense of citizenly opportunity and duty. Properly given, such instruction would be worth more for the enlargement of the pupil than anything else taught in our schools, except, perhaps, our own tongue and its literature, and the elements of arithmetic. For the needs of the commonwealth it is of the very first importance.

If we are to continue our practice of freely admitting foreigners to this country, it may fairly be demanded that those who hereafter come to us be received on probation, and that with certain exceptions, which need not here be considered, they be required within, say, three years, to prove that they can use our language understandingly, and show that they have a knowledge of the principles of our government sufficient to make them fit to dwell with us. If they fail to meet these requirements, they should be returned to their native country. To many such a demand will seem unreasonable; it will appear otherwise when we consider that we have a school system which purposes to give to all those born in this country several years of training which is primarily designed to fit them for our citizenship. The result of this and of the other influences brought to bear on those who are born here is a training which tolerably well adapts them for the needs of the commonwealth. Why, then, should we open our gates to all sorts and conditions of men, who, after the manner of the anarchists, bring into our society the pestilential notions they have come by in foreign countries? Or if an excessive idea of hospitality, or a desire for the wealth in the way of labour they bring us, leads us to receive them, why should we not take steps to bring them to an understanding of the conditions in which they have to dwell?

There can be no question that the admission of all foreigners on probation for a term of years would better the quality of the immigrants who come to us, and lead them to some understanding as to the serious nature of their duty by their adopted state. As regards the anarchists, it would force them to learn that there is another view than their own as to the nature of government, or at least the government of a true democracy. There can be no ques-

THE LIMITS OF FREEDOM 113

tion that these folk are no ordinary criminals. The fact that they are willing to die for what they assume to be the good of their fellow-men shows clearly that they have in them certain of the most important qualities of the citizen. As a class, they have been born and reared under conditions which have made it impossible for them to form any sufficient idea as to the nature and purposes of our commonwealth. Coming to us, they remain for the rest of their lives in the slums of our great cities, in that mass of ignorant discontent, as far parted from our wholesome American ways as they were in their native misery. If they could be forced to hear the truth of our institutions and ideals, there would be a chance to turn the value which their self-devotions proves to good account.

There is another aspect of the question as to the freedom of speech which should be of even greater concern to our citizens than that relating to the anarchists' teachings. Since the beginning of the Spanish War many misguided persons, animated by that frothy patriotism which wars, along with their other evils, are apt to breed, have undertaken to crush out all opposition to the policy of the government by a system of fierce denunciation of certain eminent citizens who have expressed their disapproval of that policy. These pretended patriots appear in all crises; they were one of the curses of the Civil War, greatly hindering Lincoln and other patriots who were endeavouring to keep the best part of our commonwealth, its liberty of speech, from the ruin which the strife threatened to bring about. Then, as now, these enemies of free speech were characteristically non-combatants; for men who are willing to do the unhappy duty of the citizen in arms are commonly generous-minded to those who oppose them. Since we set about our war with Spain, though the contest was, so far as the military danger went, of a trifling nature, these uncitizenly people have been more rancorous than ever before in their opposition to the freedom of speech. Their despotic motive has led them to advocate the suppression of certain newspapers that criticise the government; and one of the abler of their spokesmen, a well-known clergyman, has arraigned by name some of the most admirable of our citizens who have vigorously opposed the present administration as moral abettors of President McKinley's assassination.

The state of mind of these people, who thus endeavour by denunciation to suppress the right of men to state their beliefs, is far more dangerous than that of the anarchist. That sect is made up of ignorant foreigners who are in no sense the product of our institutions. But these who would make an end of debate are Americans of our best social class. They have had a chance to gain the spirit of our commonwealth. That they have not done this, that they retain the despotic motive, is

THE LIMITS OF FREEDOM

unhappily proof that a considerable remnant of our folk have not been brought up to the plane where they understand the nature of liberty.

Along with his insistence that he shall have the right to speak his mind on all public affairs, the citizen is bound to demand the same right for his opponent. In fact, these rights are bound together; for if it belongs to the man of only one side in the debate, it is a privilege, and not a right at all. And there is a mighty difference between the two. A despotism gives political privileges; a democracy confers rights.

It might well go without saying that there are certain limitations and decencies in debate and criticism which, if they be not observed, may fairly deny those who fail to observe them a hearing. As a man is not allowed to offend his neighbours with profanity or ribald talk, so those who use public speech so as to provoke men to crimes, or for no other evident purpose except to insult their fellows, may fairly come into the hands of the police. Yet it is well to be more than careful in all steps which shut men's mouths or stop their pens. It is well to remember the habit of the Mussulmans, who, when they see a bit of paper beneath their feet, will carefully lift it to see that perchance they may not tread on the name of God.

As a result of the assassination of President McKinley, it has been proposed to make yet other startling departures from our established customs, — changes which would introduce a new spirit into the relations of our people to their magistrates. The first of these is that the President of the United States should be protected by a special body of guards, who would see to it that he was not approached by unknown people, so that he might be saved from assaults such as have cost the lives of three out of the twenty-four men who have held that office. Such protection, though at first sight it may appear to be reasonable, would be very hurtful to the best interests of the country. It would establish the new principle that our magistrates are to be set apart from our people, and are not their fellow-citizens to whom certain duties are for a time delegated. That they are in danger is, though regrettable, a matter of no great moment. Their risk is no greater than that of soldiers in time of war, or sailors at all times. It is like that of the railway engineer or the policeman. Moreover, if our presidents are to be guarded by armed men, we may soon expect a demand for like protection from the secretaries of departments, from the governors of our states, and others in high authority. We may be sure that such a system, even in its beginning, would be a serious blow to the spirit of our democracy.

In this question of protecting our magistrate, we may well take a lesson from Queen Elizabeth, — that valiant woman who, more than any other English sovereign, except, perhaps, Alfred the Great, shaped the temper of our people. Owing to the troubled conditions of her reign, her conflict with the Roman Church, and with the Scottish queen, Elizabeth, through nearly half a century, was in constant danger of assassination. Many attempts, indeed, were made upon her life, but she met them all with an admirable equanimity. On one occasion, when in her barge upon the Thames, she was fired at, the ball passing through the arm of the rower in front of her. She took off her scarf, bound up the man's wound, and bade him go on with his work. To the frightened ambassador of France, who was by her side, she said that it was an accident, and that she would not think worse of her people than a mother of her children. She set the culprit free. Again, when a servant-woman of Queen Mary, who was half insane with grief for her dead mistress, tried to kill Elizabeth, the queen refused to have the offender punished, but sent her to her friends in France. Against the protests of her ministers, during all her reign she kept in her household many Roman Catholics, — people who, as a class, were her enemies, and from whom she must have expected danger. She, a woman of three hundred years ago, in a realm that was little better than a despotism, bore herself thus valiantly, in order to establish the principle that the head of the state should trust to its people for protection.

Again, it is proposed to have the punishments awarded to those who conspire against or attempt to kill the President of the United States other and severer than when the assault is on ordinary citizens. The objection to this course is like that mentioned in the case of the proposed presidential guard. It would tend to set our magistrates apart from the body of the people; to make their lives seem more sacred than those of common men. Thus guarded, the man would at once be distinguished from the body of our citizens; his title would not be changed, but in so far he would be by his exceptional position a king.

It would hardly be worth while to discuss these propositions to change the spirit of our relations to magistrates, save for the fact that they throw much light on the dangers which in all crises beset a democratic government, — dangers due to the fact that many persons, when moved by some grave accident, are disposed to abandon the calm judicial state of mind which the control of such a government requires. They at once jump at the conclusion that violent and revolutionary remedies are required, and are prepared to go straight away to despotism for the sake of temporary safety. These people are a menace to democratic institutions; the true citizen must be prepared to oppose them. We can best do so by showing how our commonwealth withstood the stress of the Civil War, living through the

THE LIMITS OF FREEDOM

greatest storm that has ever beset a modern state, coming out with all its institutions unharmed, and this because a host of true patriots had built it well and cared for it faithfully. It has to be confessed that a large part of the folk who dwell with us and have the semblance of citizens cannot be trusted to maintain the state. So it has been since the beginning, but the strong men have always had the strength to maintain our liberties, putting the weak aside. These makers and holders of the commonwealth are accustomed to count their lives as of small account when compared with that of their people.

CHAPTER VIII

THE CITIZEN AND THE LAW

IN political parties we see the instruments by which, through the state and federal legislatures, the laws are made, and means provided to carry them into effect. We now have to consider the attitude of the citizen to these laws as they control or limit his actions. These two sides of citizenly life — that of the law-making and the law-abiding man — are most intimately related.

Law began long before men had a name for it. In its original form it was nothing more than custom or usage, — in a word, what a man had a right to expect from his fellows: traces of it indeed are seen in the creatures below man, — as in the dogs, which know their own food and learn to keep their jaws away from that of their masters. In the next human step law is traditional; it rests on the sense of justice, and is shaped by the memory of what has been done before in like circumstances. The chief, the ancient king, or the cadi of the "Arabian Nights' Entertainment," were originally the judges; any man in power gave judgment as occasion demanded, because such work belonged with author-

THE CITIZEN AND THE LAW

ity. Gradually, as the states grew larger, — became, indeed, true states, — the kings had men to help them, and these associate judges gradually came to do the whole of the task. Thus, in England, one of the upper courts, the most ancient of them all, is called the " Court of King's Bench," though the king for centuries has had nothing to do with it. In that country, as in many others, justice still is in theory supposed to come from the sovereign.

For a long time in the history of our legal system, which is derived from the English, the laws were in part those which existed in tradition, and in part those which were put forth by the sovereign, or by the parliaments with the sovereign's consent. When our American Revolution began, the crown still had the right, with the consent of the council, to grant charters and various kinds of patents, the action resting on the assumption that the sovereign was the source of all authority, the individual embodiment of the national life and strength. The ancient traditional regulations were termed common or customary law, the others statutes. At present this division has little more than historical value. In the United States, generally with slight exceptions, all the law, however it has come to us, is now laid down in statutes which have been voted by our legislators or by the federal Congress.

In considering the matter of law, it is well to begin by noting that the greater part of the rules which guide the decent, well-behaved man in his relations to his fellows are not, and never have been, laws. As he goes about the ordinary business of life, such a man shows a consideration for his neighbours: he treats them with becoming respect; he is charitable to them in their need; he will help or defend them if they are in danger. If a house is on fire, he will, as a matter of course, do what he can to save it; if his neighbour is drowning, even though he be his enemy, he will rescue him at the risk of his own life. Such things are done not only by the better men, but even by many of those who have been, or deserve to be, in the penitentiary; they are done because to do them is an essential part of the human quality. Moreover, the nobler class of citizens — those who are the foundations of society — will not lie to help themselves; they will take care, so far as they can, that the gratification of their personal desires do not harm or even offend their neighbours.

It is the unwritten law of every realm that makes human society possible; it was that body of sympathetic usage which laid the foundations of civilisation. So complete and effective is it that men may live their lives through without knowing by experience that there is any other method by which actions are controlled. It is from a sense of the strength of this natural law that the better kind of the nihilists conclude that there is no need of any

THE CITIZEN AND THE LAW 123

other regulations than the simple, unwritten rules which guide conduct; they therefore propose to abolish all formal laws and all punishments for offences. The question is why are they wrong in this opinion. The answer is easily made: it rests upon the long and bitter experience of all peoples; the question, indeed, could only be seriously asked by those who are ignorant of the history of man.

The greater number of men, probably, in our ordinary American communities, at least nine out of ten, possibly ninety-nine in a hundred, need no other check on their conduct than is afforded by their natural and noble desire to stand well with themselves or their fellows. Unfortunately, the damaging remnant, the tenth or the hundredth man, is, as the people of old would say, possessed of the devil, or, as we now understand it, has been retarded or turned back to the place of the primitive savage, or, at least, so far back on that way that he cannot be trusted to the guidance of his desires or to the opinion of his neighbours. He is likely to murder, steal, or otherwise outrage the rights and peace of his society. It is for these unhappy exceptions among men that the machinery of the criminal law has to be maintained.

The aim of the criminal law of old was to punish, and this with such severity that the man who was tempted to become an offender might be withheld from crime by the sight or knowledge of the torments to which criminals were subjected. The most dreadful chapters in the history of our race are those which set forth the story of the tortures which were inflicted on men for slight offences. Only two centuries ago men were hanged for stealing to the value of a few dollars; cut into bits for treason, which might have been some petty attack upon the ruler; burned for differences of religion, or for the mummery called witchcraft, or tortured to make them confess what their jailers desired to have them say. In our time the tendency is to look upon the criminal as an enemy of society, but also as a miserable unfortunate, who, even in his punishment, should be dealt with in as kindly a way as may be consistent with the object of deterring others who may incline to repeat his crime. This lenient course has evidently not tended to increase the proportion of criminals to the population, but rather to lessen it, so that it is justified not only by humanity, but by expediency as well.

In another regard our modern, and particularly our American, treatment of criminals has been much less successful. This concerns the speed and efficiency with which offenders are brought to justice. In this regard our system is in most of the states in a very bad way. There is an old and eminently just rule that every care must be taken that the innocent may not be adjudged guilty. With the gain in mercy which has gone on with the centuries, new protections have been thrown about the accused, until in this country, at least, it is often very hard to secure the punishment of criminals charged with grave offences, provided they have the money to spend in having their cases taken from court to court, through all the complicated paths of the law. The result is that the people, with a rude sense of justice, along with a remnant of savage brutality which marks the newly settled portions of all lands, are apt to resort to what is termed lynching, — that is, the summary execution of the offender without any trial.

Every citizen should do all that he can to help to bring offenders to justice, and this as speedily and surely as possible. He should use his influence to have the punishments so ordered that they may not be unduly severe, to the end that the judges may not hesitate, as they sometimes do, to apply them. Here we come upon the question of the fitness of the death penalty as the price of murder, treason, and a few other grave crimes. Is it proper for the law to take life in order to deter men from these acts? This is a question which the young citizen is pretty sure to have forced on his consideration; one to which it is hard to give a well-judged answer, but for which he may prepare himself by the following considerations.

It is easy to see that the death penalty for murder is the last survival of a system in which almost all offences above the grade of small thieving were thus punished. In succession the minor offences have been brought into the list of those which were met with fine and imprisonment; even treason no longer with us brings men to the gallows; not a man was hanged at the end of our Civil War for this offence. The result of this mercy has been no increase of crime. Where the death penalty for murder has been abolished, as has been the case in certain states, it is doubtful if it has led to any greater insecurity of life.

There is another reason why the citizen may well set himself against the slaying of men by the law which has for its first purpose the protection of life. This is the uncertainty which often exists as to the guilt of persons who are accused of murder. At the present time the writer knows of two men who are charged with a most fiendish murder of a woman; have been found guilty, and are sentenced to be hanged. A careful review of the evidence leads to a grave doubt as to their guilt; yet the natural indignation of the people where the offence was committed has led to the swift and willing conviction of the accused. If these men are executed, it is quite possible, as has occurred in many other instances, it will turn out, by the confession of some man who is about to die, that they were innocent of the crime. In this case the law and the people who carry it out will have been guilty of the very

THE CITIZEN AND THE LAW

offence they are seeking to punish. A sentence to imprisonment for life, though itself a grievous thing to impose on a man who is innocent, affords a chance for correcting mistakes such as are due to strange accidents of evidence or the passions of the jurymen.

Much importance is by some attached to the argument that the state, being no more than the assembled people, can have no right to take life, for the reason that it can have no rightful powers which the individuals have not. This view seems to be mistaken, for the reason that the individual has no more right to fine or imprison people than he has to slay his fellow-man; yet some punishment must be inflicted by the government on the evil-doer. This argument would lead to the quicksands of nihilism; we should be brought back to the savage state where each man did vengeance on those who wronged him or his kindred. Moreover, it is clear that the preservation of society is a more precious matter than the life of any of its members. If the citizen is of the opinion that the safety of the people demands the death of criminals, he may well assume that the government has the right to take the lives of those who are adjudged guilty of offences against it, as he must assume that it has the right to require good citizens to give and take death on the battlefield. There can be no question, however, that the abolition of the death penalty, if it can be safely done, would make our criminal law much more reasonable than it is at present. Of old, the theory was that the penalties applied to prisoners were for punishment; in our better day we look to the treatment of malefactors as a means of reforming the unhappy men. Capital punishment is thus an inconsistency in our legal system, — a place of all others where we need to have a logical order of action.

The citizen should do all that he can to try to bring a better order into our methods of dealing with crime; he should reflect upon the nobility of the modern view, that the criminal is likewise an unhappy man, who, by his nature, is cut off from the best that life has to give him, — the sympathy and respect of his fellows, — and that along with the effect to deter others from crime should go the endeavour to help the unfortunate to a better way of life. The problem is, on many accounts, the most serious of all those the citizen has to face; he may be sure that in it lies opportunities for much improvement.

The criminal law, though in certain ways the most important part of the justice which rules mankind, is not that which most immediately affects society, for the reason that it touches only on the lower and defective members of the great brotherhood of man. Akin to it are two other branches of the law with which, in one way or another, all men have some contact; these are the public charities and the law

THE CITIZEN AND THE LAW 129

of property. The first-named of these, charity law, is a relatively modern element in our states; the second, property law, is as ancient as that concerning criminals, and is peculiarly the product and support of civilisation.

Charity law arises from the recognition of the people that a large part of mankind is weak, and thus incompetent to provide for its daily needs; that all are born with the need of incessant care in their youth; that nearly all, even in their time of strength, are liable to disabling illness, and that those who live to old age return, as it were, to infancy. Moreover, that along with the criminals and those closely related to that class in the need of peculiar care, are found idiots, and those crippled in mind or body, the natural paupers, and the insane. These unhappy folk were in early times conceived as having no rightful claim on the state; such protection as they might receive came from the charity of the abler citizens, to whom alone the state was supposed to owe any protection. The very great extension of sympathy which has come about in the last two hundred years has led to the sense that the people as a whole owe a decent protection to all who fall by the wayside. Private charity still has its place, but the insàne are no longer chained in jails or the paupers compelled to beg their bread from door to door; the law provides them a safe, though it be too often a rather stern, refuge.

This system of legal charities may be said to have its most general form in the laws concerning children. Though the youth of the land are intrusted to the affectionate care of their parents, or, in their stead, their other kindred or guardians, the law remains watchful over them; it requires that they be schooled, and usually limits the age at which they can be employed in mills and at other hard labour. In cases where children prove criminals at an early age, there are in many communities officers appointed to see that courts do not sentence them to prisons, but send them to reform schools, where they may have a chance to recover from their tendency to return to the savage or brutal state. In this way the law acknowledges that crimes may be, as they doubtless often are, only the result of the diseased or undeveloped state of the offender.

In all well-regulated societies, unfortunately as yet in only a part of this country, the idiots, as well as those who are defective because they are deaf and dumb or blind, are provided with sufficient asylums, where they may be cared for and trained so that they may have the best chance of comfort and happiness. Still further, those who, because of their defects, cannot earn their bread, are provided with simple homes, where, either in country households or in public barracks, they are properly looked after. There is in general a rule that the cost of supporting any of these incompetent people, wherever they may

THE CITIZEN AND THE LAW

be found, shall be laid on the community where they were born, or where they lived as ordinary citizens before they became unable to care for themselves. The justice of this regulation is manifest; it is the more important, as experience shows that the children of defective persons are likewise apt to be public burdens. Until recent enactments foreign countries were in the habit of sending their paupers in large numbers to this country, to its great damage; even with these laws hosts of these people find their way to us.

It has been supposed that the development of public charities would lead to a decrease in the efforts of the people to help those who needed aid. If such were the case, it would be most unfortunate, for the reason that the exercise of a wise and national charity is the best of all possible ways for developing the sympathetic motives in which spiritual culture depends. The facts do not bear out this anticipation, for wherever we find the laws of a community making the best provision for the needy, we find also that private charity is most vigorously at work in its efforts to keep lowly people from falling to the level where they will need public help, and where they may lose their self-respect by receiving it. Thus private charity, which is so guided as to prevent pauperism, insanity, or crime, is a precious gift to the needs of suffering man, — one that can come but from the fellow-man, and not from the impersonal power of the law.

It is the duty of the citizen to do all he can to develop the above-noted relation between official and private charity; he should interest himself in both these branches of help-giving, with especial care to the need of protecting the unfortunates from the great and inevitable degradation which comes upon them when they abandon the desire to support themselves; when they give up this ideal of independent life they necessarily cease to have the qualities of free men; therefore, to save them from becoming paupers is to spare the state a double loss, — that arising from the expense of their keeping, and that due to the loss of the spirit of freedom.

We come now to property law, — that branch of justice which relates to the business and possessions of men. Here we find a vast and complicated machinery designed to insure fair play in a field where the greeds are intense, and where there is the most difficulty in keeping these passions in order. Owing to the fact that property rights are easily defined, this branch of law, except for some of its smaller and more modern parts, is in such excellent shape that the citizen need not feel himself called on to do more than to accept the conditions as they are, leaving it to the jurists to better them as the need may arise. These exceptional parts of our legal system relate to certain rather modern forms of property, or to peculiar ways of holding it. Thus the plan of having stock companies which possess great properties — such as mines, mills, railways, etc. — is very modern, and the law of limited responsibility on the part of each shareholder of such a corporation, instead of the complete liability of each for the debts and actions of the other, as in the ordinary partnerships, has greatly changed the business relations of men. So, too, the combination of great financiers, or usually of several corporations, to control a particular kind of business, has introduced a new and perplexing set of questions in our government.

Although we hear a great deal about the ills which arise from trusts, syndicates, and "combines," evildoing by them has not very often been found; when it occurs, it is probably sufficiently met by laws. All corporations should be compelled to make sworn returns of their business, which should be open to public inspection. This publicity would of itself go far to bring the remedy for any ill-doing. The observer may well note that modern business is rapidly tending to methods in which one very large establishment does the work which before was done by many small concerns. The result of this is that there are fewer independent men of business and a larger number of employees for a given amount of trade. There are fewer managing men, but the business is done at less cost, and on the whole encounters fewer losses, for the reason that the men fitted to manage enterprises are rare.

Experience in many lands and times shows that the government cannot safely undertake to meddle with business methods so long as these methods are honest, and that any effort so to do is likely to result in varied disasters; the most it can do is to compel corporations to which it has given certain privileges, such as limited liability of their stockholders for debts, to make their doings public. If any citizen finds that he is captivated by the widespread notions that the government should undertake a large part of the business which is now on the hands of corporations or partnerships, — such matters as the control of railways and the sale of farm products, — he should learn of the experience in France, whereby a people who have a system of administration which is much more perfect than our own, and a rare talent for administering it, the experiment of state ownership was thoroughly tried, and resulted in utter and disastrous failure. Such a relation of state to business may in some far off time come about, but it is evident that no government in the world commands the skill which is necessary for its accomplishment at the present time.

The relation of the citizen to the laws under which he lives should be that of perfect respect and obedience to their commands. His only safe course is to assume that they represent the judgment of the majority of his fellow-voters, and that they were intended to be just. If there is a doubt whether

THE CITIZEN AND THE LAW

they are in accordance with the federal or the state constitutions, he should personally, or in co-operation with other citizens, try the issue in the courts; in the mean time he should support the statute. If the decision is against him, he has the further appeal to the law-makers, — his fellow-citizens; if he fails, then the presumption is that he is in error in his opinion as to the injustice from which he thinks he suffers. Even if he still be convinced that wrong is done him, his best course is to contend for a change of opinion among the people, remembering always that while the democratic system, with its decision by majorities under the protection of constitutions, may give rise to wrongs, there is none other in which men are as a whole so safe as to their rights.

It is not to be denied that when by some rare chance a people is oppressed in a serious and permanent way, where they are denied the right of "life, liberty, and the pursuit of happiness," and can obtain no other redress, they may honourably revolt against their oppressors; it may be, indeed, their duty to make this final protest against unendurable ills. In the United States there have been certain of these appeals to arms, all, save one, of no more dignity than belongs to ordinary riots. That of the Civil War was a revolution made, not because of any such oppression as justified the Revolution of 1776, but because the leaders of the slave states saw that they could not long maintain their local institution of slavery in face of the growing desire for its abolition in the Northern states. It was a political secession, and not in any proper sense an uprising of the people against tyranny. It may be assumed that whenever, if ever, a justifiable revolution occurs in a republic such as our own, its occurrence proves that the character of the government has changed; whatever it may be in appearance, it has ceased to be a government "by the people and for the people."

As a citizen owes respect to the laws, so he is bound to support the officers charged with their enforcement in every possible way. Thus, in case of a riot, his duty is to lend his services to the officers of the peace; in such times of need he will obey orders in the manner of a soldier. On ordinary occasions, if told by a policeman to go to his home, he would not be under any obligation to obey him; but if he happens by accident to be in a riotous throng, he should obey the command at once.

It is well for every youth to gain a knowledge of the processes of the courts of justice, as well as of the principles of the law. The first of these ends he can attain by watching a few cases tried in courts of various grade, — from that of the magistrate to that of the highest court of appeal. The spectacle he will see should, notwithstanding its simplicity, be to him very impressive, for he then beholds the greatest work of his race in the ordering of the relations between men. Unless he be engaged in some profession or calling which exempts him therefrom, — as, for instance, that of a teacher or physician, — he will from time to time be called on to serve the court by acting as a juryman. Many shirk this dignified task, but the dutiful citizen willingly makes the sacrifice. It is one of the menacing evils of our time that, especially in the great cities, so many of the citizens of capacity and education manage on various pretexts to avoid all jury duty. Thus, in this country, there is a certain military organisation not designed for the duty of the soldier, and never called on in times of need, membership of which is greatly valued, for the reason that it secures those who have it from serving on juries.

In the greater number of American states all the judges of the courts are chosen by popular election; in a few the judges are appointed by the governors, being subjected to confirmation by the state senate, or by a council. The election of judges has not been an entirely successful method of obtaining such officers; the result has been that commonly the ablest lawyers are not willing to give up their practice in order to take the office, which brings them much less money, and from which they may be ejected at any election. Men who are to give justice should not be exposed to the risks of popular clamour; it is their especial duty to protect people against "lynchings," whether the attack be on lives, property, or positions. It is unreasonable to have the criminals, or those who fall naturally into that class, and who, in certain great towns, constitute a considerable part of the voters, electing the judges who are to try them.

That our American system of electing underpaid judges has not brought greater evils than can be attributed to it, is due to the amount of latent patriotism in our citizens, and the ennobling influence of the trust which is confided to those who are chosen to give justice. There is something in the duty of deciding on the rights of people which tends greatly to uplift the character of the men to whom it is intrusted. Yet the time has come when, particularly in our cities, it is necessary that good citizens should seek to bring about a change in our methods which will take the selection of judges out of politics. The only ways of doing this are either by having the judges elected by the members of the Bar, or appointed by the governors. The latter seems to be the most practicable plan; it has, moreover, proved eminently successful in the few states where it has been maintained.

Occasionally it happens that a decision of the supreme courts of the states, as of the nation, goes against a tide of popular desire in such a manner as to defeat the will of the people. Instances of this kind are seen in the judgments in what is called the Dred Scott Case, which involved the right of the

THE CITIZEN AND THE LAW 139

slaveholder to claim a runaway slave in a Northern state; or, more recently, in the judgment of the supreme federal court in the matter of the income tax. These unpopular opinions at once lead many injudicious people to propose some action that, if carried out, would weaken or cripple the power of the court to protect the citizens against the evils that come from hasty legislative action. It was because they justly feared occasional mob-like excesses of the people, which all history shows to be the menace of democracies, that the founders of our government gave us constitutions and courts to confine them. Every good citizen who knows how his government works, recognises the efficiency of this system of protection; he sees that in the end it does not hinder the sober judgment of the people, but only its hasty action. If the people, as the result of sound judgment, desire to go by the decision of the court, all they have to do is to change their constitution. In fact, they rarely do this, because, before they have taken the many and slow steps that are required to make the alteration, they have usually come to the conclusion that their first humour was folly.

Owing to the complications of public and private business, much of the work which of old went to the courts is now intrusted to other bodies for action. Thus, in the states and the federal government, railway, harbour, land, and other commissioners have the authority to act in a judicial way. These commissioners are ancient instruments of government; they are derived from the Royal Commissions of England, but they have in recent years had a remarkable extension in this country. They are effective; and as their action can be reviewed by the courts of justice, they are not likely to prove agents of oppression.

The citizen should see how the judicial system of his country embodies the results of the long-continued efforts of men to protect themselves from injustice. To see just what the value of success is, he should read the history of his ancestors, — say, in the time of the last Tudor sovereigns of England; he will thus perceive what it means to live among a people such as our own, with strong passions, without the safeguards that well-framed constitutions and unassailable judges can give to a state. For all our gain in civilisation we, but for the majesty and power of the law, might in a day fall back into that sink of iniquity from which we have so happily escaped. When these facts are well understood, the citizen will see how absolute is his duty to strengthen and protect our constitutions, laws, and courts. He should see that changes such as are needed are slowly made and with sufficient deliberation.

It should be noted that the enemies of the social order — such as the anarchists, who seek the freedom of savages, or other dangerous men, who, while they profess to support our system, desire to replace

THE CITIZEN AND THE LAW

liberty by a method of control which shall be so slight that they may have complete license — always propose to begin their revolutions by sudden and grave changes in the constitutions and laws of the republic. When people advocate such action they need be closely watched, for the reason that, through their ignorance of the protective value of these institutions, they may endanger their safety. These prophets of violence are not newly come on the earth; it has been by watching them vigilantly and, when it was necessary, smiting them hard, that patriotic freemen have been able, through centuries of faithful labour, to build up the fortress of human rights which the law affords. Every important part of the great structure has cost the lives of thousands of patriots given on the battlefield and scaffold. It is the duty of educated citizens to make head against these dangerous people; they may be expected to appear in every party and with all kinds of projects for the good of man. The greater number of their schemes are well meant; the political schemer most often is seeking the millennium, but they are all likely to have the common stamp of ignorance as to the history and meaning of our laws. The test of the sanity of any proposed revolution in our method of government is to be made by asking whether the proposers show a due sense as to the seriousness of the task which they would undertake. It cannot be assumed that our government is perfect; it is clear that from time to time it will have to be modified to meet the needs of changed conditions, but it must be held that any such change should be made deliberately, and with the full sense that there is ever danger to be apprehended from such action.

Although it is evident enough that every commonwealth is provided with laws, and without the support they give would perish, their true meaning is not readily seen. To perceive this clearly, we have to consider certain other conditions of human action. First among these, is the fact that no man, however wise and deliberate he may be, is at all times in a state to make rules for his own conduct. If he have even a little wisdom, he knows that he must be in a law-making humour when he determines on them. He cannot do this work while he is contending with his fellow-men; when he is controlled by his greed or rage, he needs to care for it deliberately, while he has a chance to reckon what the Lord would have him do. A man who does not so frame and fix the laws which are to guide his individual action remains a savage. He is of the dangerous class, and if he does not become a criminal, it will be because those who are considerate manage to keep him straight.

The need of guiding rules is quite as great for societies as it is for individuals. This is indeed one of the first lessons that our ancestors learned. Even with the most savage peoples we find that the neces-

THE CITIZEN AND THE LAW 143

sity of having laws begins to be recognised. At first these rules are very simple: they say that no man shall slay a member of his tribe or steal his property. The chiefs strive to enforce these judgments of the people, and by so doing lay the foundations of order. With the advance from the savage to the civilised condition of society, from the little tribe, where every person knew all the others and felt them to be his kinsmen, to the larger state, where each had to deal with hosts of unknown people, it became more and more difficult to control the passions of men. Toward these strangers there was no feeling of kinship or of neighbourly regard, so that there was no protection for them against the rage and bloodthirstiness of their enemies. It needs a careful study of the history of mankind to see how very slowly and with what difficulty civilised men have managed to frame and enforce laws which would give citizens protection from evil-doers. Only a few tribes out of the thousands that exist or have passed away attained to this stage of order, and so entered on the way of civilisation. The greater number perished mainly for the reason that they did not have the citizenly motive which was needed to shape laws and make them efficient.

In our own Germanic race, including the English and the Germans, and other related peoples, we see that it has required about three thousand years to build the system of laws which protect the rights of men in their lives and property. The growth has been very slow and often interrupted by wars, which always set back the good work. That we have won so far is due to the fact that in every generation there have been men who saw that law was the very breath of the national life, and were willing to devote themselves to its preservation. It is to these myriads of true patriots that we owe our laws and the commonwealths they have made.

Ages of experience have shown that there are two classes of evil-doers, lawless people from whom the commonwealth has to fear. The one is made up of the natural criminals, — those persons who, because they have not advanced beyond the savage state of mind, or have become degraded, cannot be trusted to respect the persons or the property of other men. This group is easily dealt with by punishments. In the old days, up to within about two hundred years, such malefactors were generally executed. This method, though it has the advantage that it tends to root out evil by destroying the stock that produced it, was, as before noted, too cruel to be continued; so we now, save in very exceptional cases, endeavour to reform the criminal, or at least allow him to live. The other evil of lawlessness is found where people, on the whole decent citizens, who generally may be trusted as individuals not to harm their fellow-men, when excited by the lawless acts of some malefactor, become seized with the mob

THE CITIZEN AND THE LAW 145

spirit and proceed to slay him, often with hideous cruelty. This form of crime has always been found much more difficult to control than the other, for the reason that it is due to a certain kind of insanity that for a time turns reputable men, and even women, into brutes, so that thousands may engage in the iniquity. There can be no doubt that this form of murder by a mob is far more dangerous to our society than all the offences of ordinary villains. For it leads people by nature citizenly to lose all respect for the law.

That respect for the law which exists in our race has a somewhat curious origin. In the old days the king was supposed to be the fountain of justice, and all laws of his making. His right in this, as in other matters, rested on the idea that he was appointed by the Lord for such work. Thus it came about that the law with our ancestors had an evident sanctity, in that it was sent down to them from their respected rulers, and with the stamp of overruling providence upon it. Thus our people came of old to look upon law and justice as sacred, not so much because of what they gave in the way of safety, but for the reason that they seemed to be sent down from a high place. When, from the idea of laws being made by superior beings, we came to the democratic view of the matter, — which is that they represent the will of the people, — it was to be expected that the ancient reverence for these institutions would, in part at least, be lost. For if these rules of conduct are but the expression of the judgment of folk as to what should be done in particular conditions, it seems natural enough that they should put them aside when they have a mind to. Those who doubt the success of democratic governments such as our own find just here the basis of their criticism. They do not believe that a people will have a clear enough sense of right to submit in times of excitement to laws which they have made themselves, and to maintain these laws as sacred. These disbelievers in popular government find proof of their judgment in the extent to which mobs do their work in this country. It is for the true citizen to disprove this by showing that the people of a commonwealth such as we have may reverence and guard the law even better than those of an imperial state.

When a citizen finds himself in a position where he has to contend against the mob spirit in himself or others, he should see plainly what the law means. He should remember that it embodies not only the deliberate sense of justice of his people, but it also affords the sole means, as centuries of experience have proved, by which this justice can be made good. He should see that every man is in danger of being falsely accused; few persons, indeed, who live a long and active life are likely to escape from false charges due to misunderstandings or enmity. The only way that any man can be certain of having justice done him is by being sure of a fair trial. The first aim of the law is to secure this; and not until our ancestors devised the system of judge and jury, pledged to do justice, did men escape from the danger of the gravest wrong this world can inflict, — that of being punished for crimes of which they were innocent.

When facing the evils of the mob spirit, the citizen should also set clearly before him the fact that whatever be the crime the person has committed, those who illegally slay him are murderers. It does not help their position to say that they detest the sin and therefore smite the sinner. To see the delusion of this plea let us consider a case that illustrates it. Let us suppose that a criminal is on trial before a court and in a way to have justice done him. If hatred of him or his crime justifies mob violence, the right thing to do would be to seize him and hang him at once; as yet, those who would excuse mob law have not gone so far as to invade the court-rooms and slay men who are on trial. But there is no moral difference between such action and taking a prisoner from jail, or from the constable, in order to lynch him. As soon as a man charged with crime is arrested, he is in the hands of the law; this is true whether he be taken by officers or by plain citizens, and it is the duty of every man to see that the accused is protected until he has justice done him.

It is well also to see what are the consequences that come upon a people when they have been accustomed to take the law into their own hands. There is a good instance of this in certain parts of eastern Kentucky and West Virginia. The inhabitants of this district are of old American stock, whose ancestors were from England, Scotland, and the north of Ireland. In origin they were excellent folk, and they still retain very admirable qualities. For two generations they were small farmers and lumbermen, living much in the manner of our ancestors of centuries ago. Owing to the disturbances of the Civil War and the years after it, the laws were not enforced, and men formed the habit of each for himself doing what seemed to him to be justice on his enemies. The result is that for forty years these people have been under a reign of terror. Efforts to re-establish the courts have failed, for the judges were assailed and even slain, and the juries, for fear of their lives, have not dared to convict criminals whose guilt was perfectly evident. In a word, this people has fallen back to a state of savagery from which there seems to be no way of lifting them. Such instances show how not only civilisation, but the safety which enables men to do their simplest tasks, depends upon a faithful adherence to the law.

Those who have watched men possessed by the mob spirit have seen a quality of human nature

THE CITIZEN AND THE LAW

which is hidden in their civilised life. At such times they no longer act as rational beings, but as a herd of animals when they are moved by some contagious impulse. They are no longer rational beings, but wild beasts. When men are crowded together and any of them become influenced by rage, the fire is apt to spread to the throng, destroying all that makes the citizen the calm, judicious man who looks before and after the moment of his action. At all times we have to be on the watch for dangers that abide in the depths of men's souls, especially for the cruelty and bloodthirstiness of the savage, which lives on, though it be hidden by the habits of civilisation; but the danger is greatest in the crowd, for there, as is well proved, the old demons find it easiest to regain their ancient rights.

When the citizen finds himself called on to resist a mob, he should hear such a call afar off; his duty is plain, — it is to support the law of which he is by birthright an officer. He should straightway offer his services to the constituted authorities who are seeking to maintain justice, and take with him to this task all of his neighbours whom he can move to citizenly duty. When his services are accepted by these officers he becomes a soldier, and takes his orders from those chiefs. If he is called on to fire on the mob, he may do so with the conviction, supported by endless experience, that persuasion is vain, that death alone will break its purpose and save the law. He has no more right to flinch in this duty than in a line of battle. It is a bitter thing to slay one's fellow-men, but it is the part of the true man so to do when he is protecting his commonwealth. It is far better that they be slain than all the hard-won gains of law be lost.

In order that the citizen should be ready to support the law as a soldier, he should, in the manner of his ancestors, provide himself with suitable arms, — best a rifle of the kind used by the organised militia of his state. He should keep his gun and ammunition in order for immediate service. It is his right and duty to make him thus ready for that soldier's part of citizenship which is in every able-bodied man. Except he goes as an armed man to support the officer of the law, he should carefully avoid all throngs which are likely to become mobs; for all who swell those crowds add to the danger of the insanity that leads to those outbreaks. The leaders feel that those who are behind them are with them. Moreover, the defenders of justice are apt to shrink from firing on the crowd because they fear to kill innocent people. On such occasions the only place for the true citizen is under the orders of the sheriff or other officers of the law.

Many persons who are at heart willing enough to risk their lives in supporting the law, have an idea that, except they be members of the organised militia, they have no right to take on the duties of the soldier. This is a very grave mistake; for one of the fundamental principles of our government is that every able-bodied, honest man is a member of the militia, whether or no he be enrolled in some company. In most instances of mob outbreaks the would-be murderers know that it will take hours or days to bring an organised military force to resist them. They feel that they can easily deal with the sheriff and his few helpers, but if they saw armed citizens gathering in great numbers to his support, the effect would be mightily deterring. What we need above all in this peril is the moral effect of plain un-uniformed patriots going straight forth from their homes, if needs be, to die for the sake of justice, knowing well that if they so die it will be as nobly as those who fell at Concord Bridge or Gettysburg.

CHAPTER IX

WEALTH — ITS ORIGIN AND DISTRIBUTION

THE citizen who considers the state of affairs about him is quickly brought to dwell upon the question of wealth, its origin and distribution, and the ways in which it may be made to serve the interests of man in the most effective manner. To fit himself to understand these problems so far as they need be understood by those who care only to have the share of such learning which the voter needs in order to use his franchise wisely, it is not necessary to read many books. Even better than the use of very many books, though they aid in the task, is a little reflection on the nature of wealth, which every one can make for himself with a little help from watching what is going on in the business world about them.

We readily see that by far the greater number of the labourers in any community are paid wages for doing work which is contrived by those who give them employment. Where they are engaged in a profitable way their labour produces something that sells for more than it costs; the difference in general is usually not very great, for a large part of

WEALTH

the investments that are made result in loss of money. The gain that is made in the successful ventures is an addition to wealth; it is represented in the hands of the winner, either by so much cash in hand, or by a credit with bankers, which at will can be turned into money. The loss diminishes the wealth of the world.

The above statement gives the simplest case of business profit. There are many variations in the nature of the transactions, as where a person does his own work and sells its product. In this case any gain beyond his expenses of living and keeping up his place of business is a gain in wealth. Let us suppose that a number of people build a railway. If they operate it at a profit above the cost of maintaining it, including, of course, the ordinary interest on the investment which they have made, they accumulate a share of wealth which they would not otherwise have obtained. A man or an association of them may send a ship to sea; the chances of the deep may give them something of profit after the expense of charges and insurance are paid; this, too, is wealth gained. Yet, again, the inventor or the writer may produce a machine or a book which, by the laws, is his property for a number of years, and may give large returns; this is perhaps the most direct form in which wealth may be acquired, unless it is where a man, by his good fortune or skill, discovers a valuable mine and wins money from it.

The essential quality of wealth is that it gives the holder of it the power to call on others for labour or goods, or rather to tempt them to do his bidding. This attitude of the employer is held by all who have money to spend, whether it be but a dollar or a hundred millions. The normal and usual way in which a man comes to have a large share of this profit that may be had out of labour, is by his ability to see how labour can be employed in a way that will yield an unusual profit. This kind of foresight, when combined with the willingness and the capacity for labour, makes the able business man. We are so accustomed to see successful men of affairs about us that it is easy to overlook their value or their importance to the state. They are, however, the characteristic product of civilisation as well as one of the principal agents in the development of that complication of actions. To them and to their predecessors we owe the accumulation of all the wealth which serves to give employment to labour, and to enrich our societies. This they have done by their skill in managing enterprises so that they may win a profit from their operation.

If, as is evidently the case, there would be no large amount of accumulated wealth, except for the work of the men who have the skill necessary to create it, it is further evident that we must take care to develop these people and apply their powers. To do this they must have some effective inducement to devote their lives to their toil which is required to effect the result, — to win profit. We have only to look about us to see that no man does this work without reward; it is indeed characteristic of men that they will not often labour without some evident chance of gain. We may wish it were otherwise, but we have to take human nature as we find it. The only way which has been found, or which is likely to be discovered, to tempt able men to do business, is to give them the usual reward for such doing, — the profit that comes from the transaction; or, what amounts to the same thing, to have them at salaries proportionate to the skill which they put into the care of business. This wage, if a man have a talent for managing railways or other great enterprises, may amount to as much as fifty thousand dollars a year. This in very brief is the story of wealth as regards the conditions of production; while any industrious and able-bodied men can do a little of wealth-getting, not one in ten thousand is by nature able to do the work of creating or preserving wealth in a large way.

Very often would-be reformers come before the public with schemes whereby they claim that the uneven distribution of wealth may be avoided and all made alike rich in worldly goods. On examination we find that these schemes, if carried out, would result very quickly in making all men alike poor. In practically all cases these people who propose to recast the government are those who are born with incompetence for business, as is shown by the fact that they have been unable to win their way to success. It is therefore reasonable to believe that they would fail in an attempt to do the colossal business required to set the affairs of men on a new footing. They are, moreover, ignorant of the experiments of this kind which were made during the socialistic revolutions of France and elsewhere, all of which have resulted in failure. They do not know the history of business and are therefore as incompetent to deal with the mass of it which makes the state as a physician would be to practise medicine who knew nothing about the human body. They are also ignorant of statistics, and thus fail to see that a perfect distribution of all the wealth in this country would only for a very brief time diminish the needs of the poor; at the most it would give each person a few hundred dollars which, in the case of the greater number of them, would be quickly wasted because of their lack of economy and their ignorance as to the kind of care which their capital requires for its preservation. Let us suppose that to-morrow an absolutely even distribution of all our wealth, lands, houses, and other kinds of goods could be made, and that some omnipotent, benevolent despot presiding over the work kept this action from disorganising society, as it certainly would do except for almost superhuman control, and that thereafter things went their way as before. It is easy to see that in a few years the natural business men — those who have the ability to care for money — would gather this wealth, or what of it had not been wasted in unprofitable work, again into their hands. If by some rule they were forbidden to do this, the result would be to impoverish the whole country, reducing the people, so far as wealth is concerned, to the level of barbarians, constantly exposed to want by the failure to have a store of earnings for their times of need.

The most plausible scheme for getting rid of individual wealth, and thereby enriching the whole people, is that by which the government should own all the property, and that it should employ every one at a like wage, guaranteeing that all should have enough to live on. The objection to this project is simple; it is that government work cannot be done in a way sufficiently economical to make money. It has never been so done, and with human nature as it is, we may be sure that it never will be thus done. The man whose pay is to be the same, whether he succeeds or fails, will not and cannot work as though success or failure depended on the toil and care which he gave to his task. Done by the government, work is often excellent in quality, but it is never economically performed. If all the business of the people were carried on in the manner in which our national administrative tasks are executed, the result would be that no saving would accrue; the wealth now existing — that is, the remainder after the labourers are paid — would soon be eaten up, and general impoverishment would ensue. In other words, very soon after a check was placed on the vigilance, foresight, and labour of the business men, we would, so far as wealth is concerned, return to the essential positions of savages; nothing would be laid by; there would thus be no provision for all the vast and costly work of government and education and charity.

If these views are correct, and they seem self-evident, one of the first cares of the citizen should be to preserve and develop the business motives of the people. He may regret, as the writer does, the unequal distribution of wealth, but he will recognise that in trying to better this he must take care not to shock, much less to destroy, the peculiar conditions that have led to the accumulation of wealth, for on them depends the greater part of the good we have won in our advance above the savage state. Betterment in the distribution of wealth is not only possible, but it is rapidly going on. The labourer of to-day has more comforts and securities than had the wealthy merchant or even the prince of three centuries ago. His wage in purchasing power is worth at least twice what it was fifty years ago. Every improvement in machinery, every gain in any kind of well-administered wealth, tends to cheapen the cost of living without reducing the labourer's wage. The greater the amount of capital, which is that form of wealth that employs labour, the more desire there is to start enterprises which call for labour, and the greater the demand there is for that labour, and the higher the wage of the artisans.

It is desirable that the student should get a clear notion as to the effects which arise from the watchfulness that business men have to keep over their wealth, particularly as to that which they invest for profit. Every one may notice the difference between good and bad times. In seasons of prosperity every one is employed; many new undertakings are set about; there is a plentiful demand for labour, and all men who are fit to work have their chance to earn good wages. Suddenly there comes a change, and in a month or two — often more quickly — we will be in "bad times," where there is an arrest of business. These changes are due to a loss of confidence on the part of business men; they know that it is easier to lose money than to make it, so when there is any sign of financial trouble, they at once begin to withdraw their capital, so far as possible, from risk; they turn it into safe banks or send it to some country where it is likely to be secure. They do not begin to use it again until they feel that the danger they apprehended has gone by. Such panics are extremely harmful to the trade of a country. The citizen should see how they are brought about, and do what he can to prevent them from coming.

The commonest cause of panics, that which has produced nearly all of these disturbances that we have had in this country, is fear as to the soundness or value of the money with which debts are to be paid. It is in the nature of the business man's occupation that people should owe him money. It is essential to his safety that he should be sure as to the value of this money; if he has reason to fear that he will be paid in dollars of less value than those he sold his goods for, he will prefer to keep the goods; or if he is a manufacturer he will quit making goods until he is again certain of what he is to receive for them. Such a prudent man of business hoards his capital in times of panic, and, if possible, keeps it in the kind of money which will be good in all countries, — that is, in gold, or notes that are certain to be paid in coins of that metal.

A familiar instance of the effect of panics is seen in the use of foreign capital in this country. For the reason that we have many resources in mines, fields, and railways of prospective profit in our undeveloped regions, foreigners are in the habit of lending much money — in the aggregate hundreds of millions of dollars — to American men of enterprise. As soon as these people of abroad begin to doubt as to the kind of money they are likely to

WEALTH

receive, and fear that they may have back less value than they loaned, they cease to be willing to loan further, and try to get back that which they have sent to us.

All those who desire to increase the share of wealth which falls to the labourer should endeavour to prevent the occurrence of panics. In those times the wage-earner is likely to use up his savings and fall towards pauperism. The man of wealth suffers also, but rarely does he encounter penury. The care and skill he brings to his business commonly enables him to save the most of his fortune; his trouble is slight compared with that of the men who depend on their daily wages. Their only chance in life is to earn steadily, put aside all they can, and so rise towards the level of the capitalist, when they will be in the safe position of men who, while they labour with their hands, have some share in the wealth that earns money.

The question of the value of the money used in trade is like other questions of political economy of a complicated nature; the different sides of it cannot be discussed here. There are, however, certain very plain facts of well-recorded history that should be understood by any citizen, and which, well understood, will enable him in this matter to do his duty. The first of these facts is that money is an invention of business men, to enable them to do their trading. In primitive times one article was exchanged for another, — so many bushels of corn for so many cattle, so many cattle for so much cloth, and so through the round of affairs. Very early certain articles, by preference those which everybody desired, which were compact, and which could be conveniently cut into bits of definite weight and marked with a stamp, came to be used as the standards of value. The only materials which met their requirements were the metals, — such as gold, silver, copper, and iron, or the mixtures of tin and copper; all these in time came to be used more or less as coins.

Gradually, as the world gained experience, the coined metals became limited to three, — copper, silver, and gold. Further on copper became used only for small change, there being no effort made to keep the coins at any particular value in relation to the selling price of the metal they contained. Thus gold and silver became the twin measures of value. From time to time, as the amounts of these metals which were mined varied, they have differed greatly in their relative value, so that the coins on their face of the same stamp would not exchange equally with each other if they were not of the same metal. Again and again adjustments have been made by changing the amount of metal used in one or the other kinds of coins. These changes of ratios have always been very hard to make, but it has been necessary to make them for the reason that people would seek to pay their debts in the cheaper money,

WEALTH

while that which was the dearer would be worth more if smelted into bullion — that is, bars or ingots — than it would be on its face value as coin.

The business world is now in much trouble concerning the measures of value, for the reason that recent discoveries of silver lodes, and the extensive mining of lead and zinc ores which yield some silver, have made the cost of producing that metal so low that an amount equal to that which is contained in the bit that is stamped with the mark of a dollar can be bought in the market for about fifty cents, while the weight of gold required to make a coin of that metal costs quite as much as the face value of the piece. To recoin the silver dollars so that they may have enough silver in them to be worth as much as the gold dollar, would give us a piece too bulky for convenience: they are indeed already too large for commercial purposes, — it takes a wagon-load of them to pay a debt of thirty thousand dollars. Moreover, the price of the silver in the markets of the world is so changeable that a recoinage that would fit the price of to-day would be likely to be out of adjustment a year hence. In fact, silver, so far as the civilised world is concerned, has become an article of commerce, which varies much in value, — as much, indeed, as other important metals.

In face of these difficulties the leading nations of Europe who control the business of the world have of late taken steps to disuse silver as the measure of value, trusting altogether to gold for that service. The fall in the market price of silver bullion has been in some part due to the fact that no civilised country now permits the owner of the metal to bring it to their mints for coinage, as they do in the case of gold. So far as they can they are demonetising the metal; that is, they are forcing it out of use as a measure of value in trade.

In the opinion of many students of the money question, this step in demonetisation of silver has been taken without due sense of the consequences, and is likely to bring for a time a considerable amount of trouble to the business world. It will be especially hard on the people of many countries, such as India and China, as well as all others except those about the North Atlantic, that cannot, for various reasons, be expected to provide themselves with gold money which they have never known, and have not the means to obtain. It will tend to cut these poorer nations off from the business of the civilised world if their silver money is brought to have no value. It is therefore a question how far this government should continue in the process of demonetising silver in accordance with the dictates of the European states, — a question of the utmost importance to our people.

If this country had attained the financial strength which it is likely to have in fifty years from the

WEALTH

present time, it might possibly force the Old World states to follow its lead in such matters as the coinage of silver; but at present, strong as we are in many ways, we have not the power to dictate action for the world. If we alone take to the free coinage of silver, we risk finding ourselves with a currency which does not rest on a firm foundation of value, and which may leave us in an unhappy position to do business with our principal customers. It is certain that if our mints are freely opened to the coinage of silver, one of the immediate effects would be that gold would disappear from use in this country; it would be shipped away to Europe, for the reason that it would be worth more as bullion than to pay debts. We would then be left with only one metal with which to do our exchanges, and that least valued in the great business centres of the world. All the disused silver of Europe would be poured into this country to pass through the mints, for the owners would by our action be provided with what they much desire, — a market for the commodity. The immediate effect of this would be what is called an inflation of currency, such as occurred during our Civil War when the government issued paper money in large amounts in order to pay its expenses, without providing any means to redeem these notes in coin. It certainly would bring about an increase of prices. If this increase were alike and proportional to the previous value of all things that are sold, the effect would be simply to give speculators a chance to make money; the condition of the people in general would not be changed. But such disturbances of values never take place in this way. The change occurs in a manner to hurt the people who work for definite pay, — the day labourers, and those who receive a salary, such as clerks, schoolmasters, and all public officers.

The effect of a rise in prices on all labouring people is that their wages rise much more slowly than does the cost of all other things for which money is paid. This is clearly shown by the records of prices in all times when the buying value of currencies has fallen; it was conspicuous during and after our Civil War. In that time, though flour was ten to twenty dollars a barrel, the day labourer was seldom paid more than he is at present, when flour is worth about five dollars a barrel. The reason for this is that labour is something which has to be used at the moment; it cannot be speculated in because it cannot be stored; it cannot be "warehoused;" money cannot be borrowed on it; it must be used at the moment. The result is that the price of labour is the last of values to rise in times of inflation.

On the other hand, in the times when the reduction in the prices of goods takes place, the price of labour is the last thing to fall. Thus, the general decline of values which has occurred in recent years

WEALTH

has not carried with it that of wages; all the people of this day are receiving substantially the wages which came to them when the paper dollar was worth only fifty cents of its face value in gold coin. The reason for this is that there are many things that tend to make people dislike to lower the wages they are accustomed to pay; not only is there great risk of strikes and a corresponding disturbance of business, but the employers find it very unpleasant to lower the wages of their employees. They know that it will give those who work for them pain, and this is something that decent men hesitate to inflict; they know also that it may bring trouble, therefore they strive to increase the productiveness of the labour they employ by skilful contrivances in the way of machinery or methods, and so avoid a reduction of wages.

It results from the conditions above noted that periods when prices rise are particularly harmful to labouring men, and through the harm which they thus inflict, to society at large. The poorer classes are then least able to save money and thereby advance to the stage of the small capitalist, where, though the man still has to work, he has money for the comforts and pleasures of life; to educate his children; to provide for old age and against calamity. To such is granted the prayer, " Give me neither poverty nor riches;" they have that which may be termed truly democratic wealth. To bring our people to this state of social development should be the object of every true citizen. He should therefore oppose all measures which tend to bring about those periods of inflation which are profitable only to that most profitless of all classes, the speculators, and which are very harmful to the body of the people on whom the strength of the state depends.

It would be out of place in this book to undertake a study of the problem of money, or to discuss the many aspects of the question as to the relative merits of silver and gold as agents of trade. It may be said, however, that this matter is not fairly a political question, but one which has been unfortunately brought into politics. From the nature of the case, its discussion and determination should belong to people who make a business of dealing with the very intricate problems connected with money. To bring these questions into politics is like bringing those which relate to the methods of commerce or to the systems of medical practice into the platforms of parties. It is often enough said that the bankers and other moneyed men are endeavouring to harm the people; demagogues call them evil names and charge to them many troubles which the state has to meet. But, in fact, the people who are trained in making money by dealing in it after the manner of bankers are most deeply interested in the prosperity of those who labour, for their only chance to obtain wealth is through that prosperity. Their

WEALTH

trade is to advance money for sound business enterprises which can only repay them by success; this success means a share of the gain to all those who have to do with the enterprises. In fact, the only people who have anything to do with business affairs, who can make any money from the business mischances of anybody, are the speculators or gamblers, who arrange their plans in such a fashion that money may come to their pockets as well by a fall as by a rise in the values of stocks or other marketable things. These people have no real relation to the business of banking.

In general, where we hear the men of any business calling denounced as unpatriotic or as pursuing a course which is injurious to the country, it is safe to believe that he who makes the charges is in error, for the very good reason that people are usually honest and desire their country's good; were it otherwise, successful countries would not exist; one and all, they are the product of devotion to honest labour of the larger part of their people. In a democracy such idle talk is particularly injurious; such governments rest upon mutual confidence, which should not be brought lightly into question. Thus, there are good reasons why we should trust in a large measure in questions of finance to those whose lives have been given to the study of the very abstruse matters connected with money, especially as to the effects which are likely to arise from hasty changes in laws concerning it.

It may well be said just here that the citizen of the greatest ability, industry, and leisure cannot expect, even at the end of a long life, to know enough concerning the extremely complicated affairs of his commonwealth to be able to found his opinions on his individual knowledge; he has largely to trust to men who have a right to an opinion because they are experts, — persons who have had a long and intimate experience in the particular business. He trusts to physicians in all that regards his own or the public health; to lawyers as regards the effect of proposed laws; to engineers in matters of public works. In fact, a man or a state that does not trust to expert advice in all serious problems is sure soon to be in a bad way. When a man begins to suspect that our doctors are poisoning their pills, that our soldiers are planning to deliver this country to a foreign government, or our bankers contriving to bring ruin to the people of any district or occupation, he shows that he is not in a condition to do his duty as a citizen. He may not be insane, but he clearly lacks the plain common-sense that teaches a man to trust his fellows to do their share in the good work of the state.

Therefore, in the matter of finance, as well as in many other questions of a complicated sort, — such as those of public education, the management of armies and navies, national engineering projects, as the proposed canal across the Isthmus of Darien, —

the citizen must see that he does not act on his whims, but on the basis of expert advice. He should not, in most instances, take the judgment of one man as sufficient; in many cases he should see what is the general opinion of the experts in the particular field. If he finds it very strongly in favour of a certain view or course of action, his duty is, unless he has complete proof of a great conspiracy, or is himself so well informed as to the matter that he feels justified in placing his judgment above that of the majority of these experts, to assent to that opinion. This, indeed, is the system on which a democracy has to be administered, for all such governments rest on the well-founded principle that the joint opinions of many well-informed and just persons is likely to be better than that of any one man, however great and able he may be.

It is easy to see that as the organisation of our commonwealths becomes more and more complicated, the need of trusting to the advice of experts in difficult matters becomes constantly greater; in fact, one of the present dangers our republic has to face arises from the risk that the voters, of whom by far the greater part are busy and uneducated men, may try to decide out of their own ignorance concerning matters, when the only safety consists in relying on the judgment of expert advisers. There is no reason to fear that this trusting to the knowledge and good intentions of his neighbours will in any way weaken the independence of the citizen. Freedom does not consist in an arbitrary determination not to be influenced by others; such a position is indeed a kind of slavery to one's self. Freedom includes as its most important part the ability to make a judgment as to the value of the opinions of our neighbours, and the ways in which they may be made the basis of our actions. The man who trusts altogether to himself puts his trust in folly.

CHAPTER X

EDUCATION, PUBLIC HEALTH, AND OTHER QUESTIONS

WHAT has already been said concerning the place and duties of the citizen may have made it plain that his fitness for the trust the state imposes on him depends to a great extent on the education he has received. In truth, no man is by birth entitled to be a voter any more than he is to be a president; the right, like most other rights, is really and honestly acquired by a process of preparation which we term education. In large part this fitting of the youth for the duties of citizenship goes on in the simple training of the household. If the life there be well shaped, he learns to be truthful, dutiful, considerate of and trusting in those about him; he gains, in a word, the development of his moral qualities, which make him ready to stand by his fellows in all the trials of life, be they great or small; but this family culture, the necessary foundation of all else that goes to the making of a man, cannot serve in an adequate way unless to it is added a fit share of the learning that the schools may give. On this account the educational system of the country is next after the state of its households the fit object of the greatest care on the part of all patriotic people.

The first aim of our schools — that which gives them the name of common schools — is to give to the mass of the people a training which will serve the needs of citizenship. Long ago, at the beginning of our democracy in England, the leaders of freedom saw that popular education was as necessary to the true freeman as arms are to the soldier or tools to the mechanic. This aim of popular schooling is some centuries old, but the first place in which it found a chance to be definitely established in the plan of a commonwealth was in this country; later on the same spirit was awakened in the Old World, and in some of the states of Europe the system has been carried to greater perfection than with us. In fact, there is now danger that the value of the training which the schools in this country afford may fall much behind that of the Old World; it is in many of our states already somewhat behind Germany and Switzerland.

The essential object of a school system is to give to all youths a sufficient amount of training to enable them to read and write and use the arithmetic which is required in common life, and as a supplement to these simple things a clear idea of geography and of general history, with a special knowledge of that of his own country. To this it is desirable to add some acquaintance with the elements of natural science, as well as some training in singing. With this foundation the citizen is ready to continue his education by reading and observation, as he needs do for all his life.

Above the primary and grammar schools, which are intended for all children, comes the high school, which meets the needs of those who are in a position to receive a larger education, either because of their greater ability, or for the reason that their parents are able to support them for a longer time in their schooling. In this grade the aim is to give the pupils a wider range of knowledge. This may well include a sound schooling in English and one foreign language in those branches of mathematics which, though they have little use in common life, are serviceable in training the mind, as well as an effective training in one or more branches of natural science. Yet above these high schools come the colleges and professional schools, which are intended for the education of that abler small minority of the people, — scarcely one in a hundred of our youths can be expected to enter them. These higher institutions are designed to carry the student to the point of extended knowledge of matters which pertain to general learning, or to some high-grade occupation, such as law, medicine, engineering, or divinity. Concerning these schools there are many large problems which interest those only who make a specialty of education; there are other educational questions in which every citizen should be deeply informed. To these we will now turn.

The principal risks which our American schools incur arise from the freedom of our institutions, and are inseparable from it. The first of these is found in the fact that the goodness of the teaching in any community must in large measure depend upon the quality of the people in the neighbourhood. In a country such as France, where all things are controlled from a central point, it is possible for a minister of education to order what is to be done in each class in any school in the realm at a certain hour; by regulating the system of appointments he can manage to have all the teachers somewhere near equally well fitted to their duties. In our republic, however, the method of local government puts the control of nearly all the details concerning the schools in the hands of committees chosen from the citizens by popular vote.

For a citizen to take his fit share in developing and maintaining the school system, he should be well educated; if possible, he should have had an extended education, such as a college can afford. Even more necessary, however, than such training is a sense of the value of the work which the schools have to do, and a sympathy with those who are devoting their lives to the task of teaching; he should recognise that it is their part to discover the

EDUCATION

natural capacities of the youth, and to give these capacities a chance to perfect themselves. He should see that the strength of the state, next after its dependence on the homes of the land, depends upon its schools, and that the service he may render to this cause is in a high measure patriotic.

In many parts of our country the public schools are in a lamentable condition. The buildings are mean and very ill fitted for their uses; the teachers are poorly paid, so that the work does not command the talent or the education which it requires in its officers. The terms are so short — sometimes not over four months in the year — that the children have too little time for an education. Commonly only the primary branches of knowledge are taught, so that the abler youths have no chance to prepare themselves for academies or colleges, and are thus deprived of the chance of obtaining a higher education. As the advancement of any state depends upon the extent to which the talents of its youths are developed and brought into use in the work of life, these defects in our system of education are of the utmost importance to the commonwealth and deserve the attention of all good citizens.

The first aim of the citizen in his care for the schools should be to secure sufficient pay for the teachers. These servants of the state deserve the same recompense that is given to those who are employed in the other professions; their rewards should be as great as those received by the lawyers, physicians, engineers, and other men of affairs; if they are less, we may be sure that in the end we shall have for this work of first importance less able persons than go to those other occupations which, though of great value, are not so necessary to the good of the commonwealth. The next important matter is the grading of the schools. These should, if possible, be so arranged that those who are fit for the higher education should be able to go up a well-made ladder of learning until they can enter those institutions which represent the highest culture, — the universities of the country; until these main ends are attained our school system must be regarded as imperfect.

The young citizen, even while but a school boy or girl, can do something to aid the noble cause of education. He can help in teaching the slower of those who are at work with him; he or she can take a share in keeping the rooms clean, seemly, and adorned as with flowers, with the result that the place, however plain it may be, if indeed it be but a loghouse, may be gracious and elevating to those who spend their days there. There is, in fact, no other place except the home where the youth can so well begin to practise the art of helping his fellows in a common cause as in the school.

Next after the school, if it be not a part of it, as an object of citizenly care, should be the local library.

EDUCATION

All homes should have some books, but the number in most households is necessarily small. There is thus always need of some public store of them whence those who read may have what they require. In every village or rural neighbourhood there should be such a public library; it will be of great value, even though it have no more than one hundred volumes, provided these be well selected. As there are in our own language a million or more of useful books, the selection needs care; but there are good lists prepared by skilful men which will serve as guides in such matters. Several instances are known to the writer where young people have associated themselves together so effectually that they have laid the foundations of libraries of great value to the communities in which they are placed.

The most important question connected with education is that of the training the individual man so that he may attain to his maximum of usefulness to himself and to others. The greatest loss from which mankind suffers is from this waste of talent. The writer has had a good deal of experience with men, not only with young people, as a teacher, but with grown men in armies, workshops, and mines. The clearest understanding which comes from his acquaintance with men is that men have rarely attained to anything like the measure of their capacities. The impression made on him is that perhaps not one-hundredth part of the talent which is offered by nature is ever brought to bear its fruit; by far the greater part of this ability lives and dies unnoticed, unknown even by those who have it. The shortest way to a new heaven and a new earth is by so contriving our methods of educating people that the work may fit its name, and result in a real bringing out of their capacities.

Properly organised, a democratic society should be much the best place among all associations of men thus to bring out the abilities of individuals. The sense of freedom, the feeling that he is able to go into any walk of life, and that his neighbours wish him success in his efforts to do what he can for himself and for the commonwealth, should serve to inspire a youth to develop the talent which is given to his keeping. It is a part of good citizenship for every young person to search with care into himself in order to find out his powers. The plain question, what am I good for? should be asked by every one as soon as he comes to discern the nobility and beauty of this world he is to work in and for; the answer is not easily to be found. Yet every one who has in him the quality to ask it seriously and persistently is fit for good service to himself and his time.

No man, young or old, can clearly see himself; to find his powers he needs the help of his schoolmasters and his abler neighbours. In general, physicians and lawyers are the best judges as to the capacities of young people, for they are, by their occupation, better trained to look into human quality than other classes of men; they have also a better knowledge of human occupations than other people. A broad-minded schoolmaster may aid a youth to know himself, but usually teachers lack acquaintance with the work of the world which is needful in order to make a man a judge as to the place he is suited to fill. The best indication of peculiar capacity is a strong desire to do a certain kind of work. If a youth finds a pleasure in helping sick people or wounded animals, it may be presumed that he is fitted for the life of a medical man. If mechanical contrivances attract him, and at the same time he has a capacity for mathematics, it is likely that he will do well as an engineer. So with the other occupations, if they distinctly attract the youth there is a presumption that his talents lie in the path of his desires.

There is to be noted that there is a certain danger that the youth may be deceived by his tendency to go with the crowd. Thus, in the recent public interest in electricity many a boy, because he has taken a fancy for making the little machines which relate to the art of that science, has got the notion that he is fitted to be an electrical engineer, and pushes towards that profession. If he enters it, he soon finds, however, that to rise above the level of the labourer he needs a very long training in mathematics and mechanics; and as he cannot well attain this education, he is likely to find that he is fixed in a low grade of mechanical employment. It must not be supposed that, because these places of the labourer in an art have to be termed low that they are by any means contemptible, but they are for those who do not have the natural ability for more important work. If a man of superior powers finds himself in such a position, he is pretty sure to become discontented; he should indeed become so, for he is out of his fit place in the work of life. It is therefore most important to avoid the risk of being led to choose a calling because at the moment it is fashionable or much in the minds of men.

If men or women are conscious of a peculiar capacity, he or she should not suppose that they ought straightway set about the cultivation of it to the exclusion of all other training. The greater this capacity the more important it is that those into whose keeping it is given should have what is well called an "all-around education." Their peculiar power should be continually cultivated; its development should indeed be the first and main aim of their training, but their minds should be broadened on every side. If a gardener have a precious seed, he does not haphazardly commit it to the earth, there to take its small chances of prospering. He takes abundant care to select the right soil and exposure by which to give the germ the best chance of developing its latent qualities; he spares no pains in the culture of the valued object.

On the principle of the more the value of the seed the greater should be the care in dealing with it, those who have in them the germs of value to themselves and the state should, by their care or by the fostering of others, be given a chance fully to develop. Thus, if a youth have a talent for invention, he should have it assiduously cultivated, and the main line of his education should be devoted to this end; he should be made strong in mathematics, mechanics, and the history of the art for which he has a taste, but at the same time he should be enlarged by general knowledge, so that his mind may not become onesided.

Intellectual training is very nearly comparable to that of the body in which the mind finds its lodgement. It is well known that our body cannot be well developed by the exercise of some of its particular parts. Thus, sailors and ranchmen, not being accustomed to walk, are likely to have weak legs; blacksmiths are strong in their right arms; even soldiers with much marching with a stiff uniform movement become in time in a way deformed. A proper growth cannot be attained by one kind of movement, — it needs a full gymnastic system to give the limbs a symmetrical development. So with the mind, which has more parts needing exercise than the body, the gymnastics for growth have to be carefully contrived. Unless this is done, the result is a onesidedness which is painful to the man and lessens his value to the commonwealth, which needs to have its citizens in their perfection.

THE CITIZEN AND MILITARY DUTY

By the laws of this country any man who is fit for the task is liable to be called on to serve as a soldier; he is, in fact, a soldier because he is a citizen. This requirement has not to any great extent been brought home to our people. In European countries, such as Germany and Switzerland, every youth has to take his turn in the army unless he has been by defects of his body exempted from such duties, or has entered into the priesthood. This obligation of military service is the last remaining of the ancient customs which placed the man — his life and fortune — absolutely in the hands of his sovereign or chief. It is easy to see that this power of the state to demand the life of its citizens for its service is sharply in contrast with other modern institutions. No state can legally take the land or other property of any person without paying him the full value therefor, yet it can at any moment demand, if needs be, his life in the support of the law or for the protection of the commonwealth. This power is not limited to times of war; any sheriff can, if he needs help in preserving the peace or capturing offenders, require at his discretion citizens to go

MILITARY DUTY

with him on his dangerous errand. If they refuse to obey him, they are liable to heavy punishments.

The law that places the whole military strength of a state at the command of the officers of the law — of the sheriffs and their deputies, or of the military authorities, the governors and president, or those they appoint as commanders — is necessary to the safety of the commonwealth. People within the state may revolt, or other nations may invade its territory, — either of these calamities may bring such ruin that it is justified in requiring those to whom it gives shelter to give in their turn their lives for the preservation of their country. So, too, the people are justified in esteeming as most honourable this willingness of their fellow-citizens to devote themselves utterly to the commonwealth.

So long as a nation is at peace, if the people be well educated and enterprising, each year sees a gain in their spirit and their substantial goods. They accumulate wealth, their homes become more comfortable and more cultivating, the sense of personal freedom grows; all the conditions of a genuine democracy have a chance to develop. When a great war comes all these influences which favour the nurture of cultivated freemen at once disappear; a large part of the population is withdrawn from productive labour and set about the tasks of destruction. A battlefield of ordinary magnitude sees in the loss of life and of valuable materials a ruin which may well, measured in money value alone, aggregate as large as that of the great Chicago fire. It is a very ordinary fight which does not entail a like ruin which is greater, measured in money alone, than that caused by the tornado which swept over St. Louis. It is safe to estimate the value to the state of the average American citizen who dies in battle or is permanently disabled by wounds at not less than five thousand dollars. Therefore in such a fight as Gettysburg, where about thirty thousand men were killed or crippled, the immediate destruction, so far as it can be measured in money, indeed, the least of the cost, was one hundred and fifty million dollars. But this reckoning takes no account of the homes made desolate, or of the widows, children, and aged who are left unprotected by the taking away of those who should have cared for them.

Great as is the commercial ruin of war, it is perhaps in importance exceeded by the moral evils which it entails. It is impossible to withdraw men from the civilising effects of decent social life and to set them about the work of war without to a greater or less extent harming them. They are for a time detached from the habits of obedience to the laws of civilisation; what control they know is the rude kind of military discipline. When, as in our Civil War, citizens of both sides entered the army with high moral purposes, their motives may save them from the worst effects of their life as soldiers,

MILITARY DUTY

as it did our good men in that time of trial; but there were tens of thousands who were so greatly harmed by that conflict that they were afterwards unfitted for their duties as citizens. Those who know best what civilisation and the true citizenship on which it rests really is, see clearly that in all men, however well established, there is still the remnant of the ancient cruel, lawless, savage motives. It needs all the good influences of family and social life to keep down these vile tendencies of men; war inevitably turns men towards the level of the beast.

It is a remarkable fact that with all these hideous evils of war many of the people of our time have a strange admiration for it and look to it as a source of national blessings. The reason for this doubtless is that they do not see that the patriotism which may be made evident by the summons to arms is really developed in the plain doing of duty for the good of one's people; that the self-devotion which leads a man to die on the battlefield is not developed in the fight, but is due to the faithful devotion to the duty of fathers and sons in the household, to the zeal and labour of the youths in school, and to the endurance of toil by which men earn their daily bread. Battles give a fine chance for the display of these qualities, but they are no more made on its fields than are the weapons which are used there. It has been the writer's unhappy chance to see something of war; it is his firm conviction that all armed struggles are monstrous ills which permanently weaken and degrade the states that wage them; that they are not necessary to train men to valour, for all men of quality meet such trials bravely, and that the first duty of the citizen is to guard against their occurrence as he would against outbreaks of pestilence.

It is easily seen that this view of war differs from that which the reader will find expressed in most books, where battles and sieges are reckoned as amongst the noblest deeds of men. The reason for this is that in the early stages of civilisation the primitive tribes and small states were engaged in almost continual war, so that the people thought of little else. The safety of their lives and property depended on the valour and skill of their men in combat; they naturally came to look upon a warlike humour as the one most important quality of the citizen; it was indeed such in that state of society. Nearly all the early literature is largely given up to praises of bravery; it is the leading motive in the most of the great classic masterpieces of song and story. This endless idealisation of warfare has led to the worship of the art. Moreover, in the olden days, when men fought their battles hand to hand, when each action was made up of a set of combats between individual heroes, war was very dramatic and had a certain effect of stimulating men to heroism.

MILITARY DUTY

In our modern warfare personal valour has relatively little place; the soldier is a part of a great machine, which acts best where it is most mechanical in its working. There is hardly any chance of individual fighting; it is rarely, indeed, that the soldier looks into his opponent's eyes, — he may go through a long and bloody campaign without seeing the enemy, unless it be the dead or prisoners, near enough to tell whether they were white or black. In these conditions war has lost the picturesque features which of old gave it a certain charm, and which served to stimulate some of the lower yet valuable qualities of men. Moreover, in modern times, when commercial and business life is much more important to prosperity than in the earlier ages, war has become vastly more destructive to the property of the people. A year of the calamity may ruin the trade of a nation for the lifetime of a generation.

Although war should be reckoned as the greatest evil, save degradation, that can befall a state, and as a misfortune which is to be guarded against in every honourable way, it is necessary for a commonwealth to be prepared to undertake it when it has to be met. It may happen that some foreign state not civilised to the point where it detests fighting forces war upon us, or that misguided people take up arms to resist the legal authorities; for such chances the citizen should be prepared alike in mind and body. This is particularly necessary, for the reason that our country is not provided with a large standing army. The existing national land forces amount to about sixty thousand men, or perhaps the twentieth part of the troops which would be required in case we had to defend the border of the United States from the danger of invasion such as would exist in case we were at war with any foreign power.

To prepare himself for the duties of a soldier, the young citizen should acquire so much of the art as he may well learn from a year or two of service in a well-drilled militia company. This service will not make him entirely fit for duty in war, but if he knows how to use a rifle or a cannon with reasonable skill, and acquires the habit of obeying orders as well as the tactics of the company and regiment, he can, in the course of a few months of active work, become a sufficiently skilled soldier.

In seeking a military training, it is well to make the most of the time and thought which it calls for. It is therefore worth while for one to study the art of war, so that, in case of need, the service rendered may be valuable. The greatest necessity in time of war is of officers who have some understanding as to the ways in which troops should be cared for, and the manner in which bodies of them may be handled to advantage. If a youth has a taste for this, a wide field of study is open to him.

In dealing with the question of war, the citizen

can be most effective on the side of sane action by reproving those politicians who think to gain the votes of thoughtless people by clamouring for trouble with foreign nations. He should bid them see that no false notions of national honour are to be allowed to lead the people into warfare any more than they lead the well-behaved man to street brawls. There is such a thing as national honour, as there is of personal self-respect. In case of need a man will resist an assault as best he may, but in no case does the decent, law-abiding citizen go about seeking for some excuse for fighting. When he finds a legislator looking for occasions which may be the basis for foreign quarrels, he may be sure that he is not fit for his office.

THE CITIZEN AND PUBLIC HEALTH

One of the most important modern gains of civilisation is found in the care which the more enlightened commonwealths take to keep the people from the inflictions of disease. Science has taught us the ways in which most maladies originate and spread. One by one the various plagues, as well as smallpox, diphtheria, cholera, yellow fever, and a number of other pests which once destroyed the larger portion of the population, have been so far brought under such control that they are either no longer known in well-regulated lands, or, if they appear, they are, by the use of proper safeguards, stamped out. Great as has been the gain, the effect of these advances in the science and art of medicine, there is still need for a large amount of patriotic endeavour in order to bring the benefits of this knowledge to the people.

It would be a low estimate to reckon the number of persons who die from maladies due to bad drainage, poisonous water, and other preventable diseases, within the limits of the United States, at a quarter of a million each year. This fearful loss of life does not fully measure the magnitude of the infliction; to it we must add the expenditure of time and money involved in caring for sick people, and the damage done by their more or less long separation from their occupations. There is no means of obtaining an accurate measure of the gravity of this burden on the commonwealth, but it doubtless exceeds in money value alone all the other avoidable expenses that are imposed upon us.

We have noted that it is the citizen's duty to make himself ready to meet the evils of war, although that infliction is one that rarely comes upon a state, and then usually because it is chosen. How much more obligatory it is for him to make ready to meet these enemies of disease which are always at his gates when not actually within them! To make himself useful for this most honourable battle, men should know something of the laws of the human body, and those of our domesticated animals, as well as of

PUBLIC HEALTH

those methods of preventing disease included under the term "hygiene." If he cannot gain this knowledge so that he may act independently, he can see to it that his community has some guidance from experts who know how diseases may be avoided. Physicians of sound training are good advisers in such matters; in many states there are boards of health which will give information and guidance in such work.

The struggle against disease needs begin in each household, where the drains, the water supply, the access of light and air, are all features which affect the life and health of the occupants. So, too, the nature of the food and the way in which it is prepared for the table has much influence on health. All these matters are well treated in many books, so that knowledge concerning them is easily acquired. If each citizen who has a chance to control the conditions of a house will attend to these matters of health, he may be assured that the work he does is in essence true patriotism, which has no higher task than that of safeguarding the households of the land.

In general, the best method of obtaining fit sanitary condition in a town, as well as for making many other improvements, is to do the work of diffusing interest and information through a society modelled on those which are being founded in many of the communities of the eastern part of this country and some portions of the west, known as village improvement associations. The aim of these clubs is to study into the needs of the place in which they are located, and to meet these needs as best it may be done. The most immediate interest of the members may well be a matter of health; but the schools, the public library, the better care of the poor, the adornment of the neighbourhood, may well command attention. Such societies enable the citizens who are alive to the needs of progress, usually but a handful in any town, to direct the action of their ignorant neighbours and prevail over their indifference to the public good.

It hardly needs be said that a care for the health of a community should begin by fit attention to one's own bodily vigour. Every person is, by his obligations to those with whom he is associated, held to take care, if possible, not only that he avoids being a burden upon them, but that all his powers of body and of mind are in the sound and serviceable state. To attain this end, he needs to know enough of the principles of right living to preserve his health and augment his strength. Even if he be born weak, he may, as the writer knows by personal experience, so manage himself that he can do the work of a man steadily up to the demands that busy life may make upon him, even to old age. A sober way of living, with due care to bodily exercise, bathing, rest, and food, will enable almost every one who survives the trials of childhood to do citizenly work that will give him the satisfaction of duty well done, and bring him the rewards of a well-spent life.

THE CITIZEN IN RELATION TO POVERTY AND CRIME

However well managed a commonwealth may be, a certain portion of its population, smaller in proportion to the goodness of the management, is certain to fall into the defective class, and prove for one reason or another unable to make a success of life. In part, these unsuccessful persons are so for the reason that their bodies or their minds, or both together, are so defective that they cannot earn a living, and they thus become innocent burdens upon the state; in part, because of defects in their moral qualities, or in the training which these qualities need, they break the laws, and, so doing, become a burden on their fellows. Both these classes of people are a load upon the state,—a load which it is difficult for the good and effective citizens to carry.

In considering his relation to the defective people, the citizen should remember that he has two duties to perform,— the one to his own better nature, the other to the public. From his individual duty he owes to all these unfortunates a keen and effective sympathy: he must help them in any way he well can; he must seek to keep them from falling, and lift them up when they have fallen. There is no distinct limit to which this exercise of Christian kindness and forbearance should be carried except that the giver must take account of the duties he owes to those who are most nearly dependent upon him, or that which impels him to save his time and means to carry out more important plans of labour for other ends which may be profitable to his fellow-men.

It is otherwise with the relations of the commonwealth to poverty and crime. Long experience has shown that the poor, if they be helped by public charity, or private, which is not directly given, are thereby debased, and are quickly fixed in their habit of looking to others or to the law for relief; that the criminal classes, though they may be treated with all possible kindness, have to be vigorously and inevitably punished, and that they have to expect no pardon except where they have earned it by good conduct while undergoing suitable punishment. The difference in quality between private charity and public is much to be regretted, but it does not seem possible to avoid it in the present condition of human nature.

In helping poor people, the true kindness is shown by those who seek to aid sufferers to help themselves, by finding work for them to do which is fitted to their needs, and by inciting them to the industry which they so often lack. In this way they may in most instances be kept from becoming dependent on

POVERTY AND CRIME

the hard provisions which the law makes for them. This and other charity best be given, not through any societies, but directly from the giver. Thus offered, it comes to the poor as a Christian human deed and has thereby a human quality that can never belong to the mechanically rendered aid of the law. So far as he can afford it, the citizen will see that the dependent people about him never lose touch with the hearts and hands of their neighbours, as they inevitably do when they are sent to the poorhouse.

As regards criminals who have endured the penalty for their offences, the duty of the citizen is not so clear as it is in relation to the poor, where all his motives should be charitable. The felon who has been discharged from prison needs aid even more than the pauper, but it is often very hard to give it to him. If his offence was of the character which is brought about by some moment of great temptation, it is clearly our duty to receive him back into society, and to do all we can to help him to live a righteous life. If, on the other hand, the crime was of a base character, we may often be sure that the man is a permanently dangerous person, who is not fitted to live among decent people; in these cases, though charity should not fail, the man should be watched for the rest of his days. The citizen needs to remember that he is an upholder of the state, and that it is to him, because of his strength, that the weak of mind, of morals, or of body have to look for their chance to be helped through life. He should therefore approach these problems of dealing with the deficient people as the strong man goes to the weak and suffering, tenderly, and with the sense that his strength belongs to all who are in need. He is to remember, however, that the safety of the commonwealth demands a course which will, so far as possible, deter the criminal from offending, and enforce on the poor an earnest striving to keep themselves in a self-supporting condition.

It is most desirable that all these persons who have to be supported by the public should be kept in a Christian manner. It is therefore better that the paupers should be placed in decent families rather than in poorhouses or in poorfarms, where the worthy and the unworthy — those who have fallen by accident and those who have sunk by lack of will or from vice — are herded together in a way which is calculated to bring pain to the sensitive inmates of such asylums.

For those to whom after an honest and laborious life there comes an old age of poverty, the proper means of support is, in the opinion of some persons, a carefully bestowed pension. The trouble with this system will doubtless be to separate those cases in which the kindred of the old are able to support them from those in which this help cannot be reasonably expected. Every argument, however, which can be brought to justify the pensioning of needy men

POVERTY AND CRIME

who have worthily served the state in war applies likewise to the cases of those who have in their prime done their best for the commonwealth in the labours of peace. To take any other ground is to give to the work of war a dignity, as compared with the duties of ordinary life, which it does not deserve.

CHAPTER XI

IMMIGRATION, UNIVERSAL SUFFRAGE, AND THE NEGRO QUESTION

THE success of a democracy depends altogether on the quality of the people who compose it; if they be of a common mind as to the main purposes of the state, sufficiently educated, mutually helpful and considerate, seeking good government, in a word, truly patriotic, the commonwealth will be strong; if there be an admixture of people who do not have these qualities in direct proportion to the amount of the uncitizenly element, the political life will be weakened, and at a certain stage in the degradation the state will cease to have the characteristics of a government for and by its true people. It is this general truth that makes the question of immigration of great interest to all Americans, for into their country there is now pouring a great tide of folk gathered from nearly all the states of the civilised world, and some that are not, in one sense of the word, civilised at all.

At first sight there is much to please us in this spectacle of folk who have suffered from the political oppression which other lands inflict upon them, seek-

IMMIGRATION

ing a refuge in the ample room of our national domain; to them and their children this country is a land of promise and often of ample fulfilment. It is indeed a noble thing for a state to be, as our own is, a place of safety to millions of shipwrecked persons. There is, however, another and very practical side to the question which every citizen must consider. These foreign people are principally from countries whose speech, customs, and ideas of government are very different from our own. This difference is not a matter of the moment; it has existed for the centuries during the time in which our ideas of democracy have been slowly forming and working into the life-blood of our folk. The greater part of the people whence our immigrants come have been blindly submissive to the will of others and are thus without any experience in self-government. Coming to us, they are not only foreign, but in a way permanently so. Except so far as we can make them over, — as it were, melt them down and recoin them with the stamp of our country, — they will remain aliens for generations to come.

In certain of the great cities of this country which have been to a great extent occupied by foreigners, the politically debasing effects of these immigrants is seen in the degradation of this government, — a degradation which seems likely to resist all the efforts of the American population to remedy. It does not follow that because foreigners lower the quality of an American commonwealth that the action is due to their vices; much the same effect would occur if they were in their natures even better as men than ourselves. The effect is mainly caused by the fact that they do not fit into our system. They do not understand our state, and all their previous experience keeps them from doing so. They cannot as a rule fall into our ways; they tend in almost all cases to form societies of their own, — little bits of alien countries which remain imbedded but not mingled in American life.

It must not be supposed that all peoples of alien birth, even when they speak foreign languages, are strangers to the purposes of our democracy. There have been many thousands of those who have come to us who were, when they came, as good American citizens as any who have been born and bred upon our soil. It would be easy to name many score who, in our own and earlier times, have so well served us that it is difficult to see how the republic could have done its work without them. But these are but exceptions; the rule is that foreigners are not at the time of their coming of a quality to meet the duties of the American citizen, and cannot be made of that quality by any process that has been as yet discovered.

The argument may be made that these people bring so much strength, skill, and general value, other than that which makes for sound government, that we should take them for their good qualities and neglect the bad. In this view of the matter we are apt to be misled by the tendency to admire bigness without regard to the nature of the mass. We are charmed by the mere growth in numbers of our population and forget that the true greatness of the commonwealth is not to be thus measured. It would be better for us if we could halve the total number and double the goodness of our citizens. We should thus grow faster in all that gives value to the state, — in intelligence, patriotism, and all else that makes for the dignity and greatness of a commonwealth.

It seems clear that to preserve the safety of our institutions, our citizens need be watchful as to this incoming of aliens from European and other lands. This cannot well be done by any general law against immigration; such a law would be inhuman, for the reason that men of the better sort, educated and high-minded, are citizens of the world. No state suffers from their presence; they therefore have a right to go about as they please. If such persons desire to cast in their lot with us, they have a just claim to a hospitable reception.

It is otherwise with the ignorant and undeveloped folk who form the peasant class in many European states. These people have not, and rarely are able to acquire, an adequate conception of the motives of this republic; its advantages to them consists in an easier chance to make a living and a certain freedom from oppressive laws. Where the incomers are from any one of a number of countries in southern Europe, they may have notions concerning government which are utterly hostile to our democracy. Thus, the Sicilians, though in many ways an admirable people, have, owing to the long-continued oppression from which they have suffered, acquired the habit of looking not to the law for protection, but rather to a secret society known as the Mafia, which guards its members from danger and from punishment. For many years the Italian government has been trying to stamp out this pernicious society, but it seems impossible to do so. Even among the Sicilian immigrants in this country this association continues in a way to give the police much trouble. It needs no argument to show that such folk are not fit material out of which to make American citizens. We cannot give them the idea of the majesty of the law on which our citizenship rests.

The best way in which to limit the coming of foreigners to our country — a way which gives promise of keeping the immigrants to something like the quality of those who have made our commonwealth — is to provide in the first place that criminals, paupers, and other defective persons shall not be allowed on any terms to enter; next, that none shall be allowed to come who are not able to read

IMMIGRATION

and write in our language or their own. This test of education is not the best that can be imagined, but it is the best that can be applied. It insures a certain better quality of people when we prove that they have a chance to know something of matters beyond the limit of mere gossip. Such a test would not to any extent hinder the coming of folk from the northern states of Europe, whence we obtain the more valuable of our immigrants, — those who have, or may quickly acquire, at least a part of our motives. It would tend to keep out the lower peasant class from such countries as Russia, Hungary, and Italy, from which we have little to expect in the way of a rough material from which to make American citizens. Such a law would do much to protect us from a very grave danger.

When the foreigner comes to this country, he should be, if possible, induced not to settle with those of his kind, but rather to enter at once into close relations with the native folk, and this in order that he may in the full meaning of that word quickly be naturalised. It has been the custom, more in the past than at present, for large bodies of aliens to colonise on unoccupied land, so that they might keep their modes of life and thought as they were in their mother country; the effect of this has been to retain them in some instances for many generations in an alien state. An example of this is seen in the Pennsylvania Germans who came to this land about two hundred years ago. Although these settlers are admirable people, closely akin to us in blood and quality, and of good ability, the fact that they have retained their old language and modes of thinking has withheld the greater number of them from the stream of American life. It is true that many of the abler persons of this interesting colony have gone forth from it and taken a full and important part as citizens, but the greater number have kept by themselves; they are faithful and excellent members of society in all but an understanding of what the country is striving for and should attain to.

When the citizen has foreigners about him, he should endeavour to do what he can to give them their full place in political life and understandings; he should give up his national prejudices against them, for such feelings serve to add to the difficulty of bringing the stranger into a proper helpful relation to the state. It is only when they gain a sense of fellowship with those about them that they begin to put off their alien state of mind. Democracy, as often before said, — it cannot well be said too often, — rests upon friendly understanding between men who share its blessings. No man can ever be introduced to it who is not welcomed thereto.

UNIVERSAL SUFFRAGE

In the beginnings of our American system of government the suffrage — that is, the right to vote

— was limited to those citizens who had a certain amount of property, the amount varying in different parts of the country. It was the theory of the founders of the republic that no man had an inherent right to vote, but rather that the commonwealth appointed him to vote because it supposed that he would do so in a wise manner. Gradually, as the democratic experiment has been carried on and the spirit of it extended, it has come to pass that the property qualification has practically disappeared, at present the only limitation being in general that the citizen shall be twenty-one years old, self-supporting, not convicted of any serious offence against the law, and of sound mind. In some states, with a manifest tendency to extend the restriction, the voter must also show that he can read and write the English language. This is sometimes called the *Massachusetts limitation*, for the reason that it originated in that commonwealth, where it has worked well in sifting out those who, if allowed to vote, would not be likely to make a wise use of the franchise.

The property qualification of the voter seems at first sight a very reasonable limitation, for the reason that almost all persons whose judgments in political matters are likely to prove of value have some income or capital sufficient to qualify them to vote under a reasonable limitation, — one that would not fix the amount of the possessions too high. But this method of limiting the suffrage has not met with favour among our people because they feel that it is the money and not the man that does the voting. The fact that it was originally in and has gone out of use is enough to show that it does not at present meet the desires of our people. It is not unlikely, however, that men may be called on to prove that they either have some wealth or earn a fair wage before they are allowed the franchise.

It is clear that the objections to universal suffrage are strong. It is evidently unreasonable to leave the decision of grave matters of public policy which may by their decision endanger the safety of the republic to people who are unable to read or write. Probably not one-half the voters of this country would be acceptable as jurymen in a case in which the trial concerned a matter where the men had to have clear and well-trained minds. What right, then, have we to expect these ignorant and untrained men to act wisely when the case is as large and difficult to understand as are most national problems? Looking at it in this way, the student is apt to feel that universal suffrage is an evil in our constitutions which needs to be cleared away in order to save the state from grave dangers.

The citizen has to learn that in all political affairs experience has much more value than theory; he therefore turns to see what are the evils that have been met in our long trial of a system of voting by which nearly every adult man has had the right to a share in public affairs. It is often enough said by those who regard universal suffrage as a great evil that the poor quality of our representatives in legislative assemblies, the defective government of our cities, the reckless expenditure of public money, and other ills of the commonwealth are due to this system of voting. The ills are indeed evident enough, but their cause is by no means so plain. We find like troubles in European states, where the suffrage is limited; they have existed in American states before they gave up the property qualification for the franchise.

Against the evil of having a large, perhaps the larger, number of our voters incompetent to reason about matters of statecraft, we may set the evident ills that would come about if the suffrage were limited to the relatively small number of people who are fit to give judgment in such matters. In this case the larger part of our citizens would at once feel that they were unrepresented in the government; they would inevitably become discontented; there would be no outlet to their dissatisfaction except in revolts, which would be pretty sure to take place. At least a moderate degree of contentment on the part of the great majority of those who live within it is a condition of the perpetuation of a republic like our own; no such society can survive with the larger or even a very large part of its citizens convinced that they are oppressed. Call it what you will, a government with a limited suffrage becomes in a way an oligarchy, or, as the word means, the rule of the few who attain political control, — a form of control which, though not bad in theory, has everywhere led straight away to oppression. It has proved worse than the method where the control is in the hands of an aristocracy, — that is, where the few inherited their rights to govern from ancestors who won it by some kind of excellence. Therefore if the suffrage is limited by requiring education, property, or both, the limitation should not exclude a large part of the citizens.

If every man who voted undertook to determine on the way in which his ballot should be cast by a judgment as to the matter in dispute; if the issue depended on the goodness of such opinions, it would be difficult to manage a state such as our own on the basis of universal suffrage; but the work is not done this way. What really happens is this: the untrained voter has a general impression as to the quality of the two or more parties which seek his support. This impression is usually in the main tolerably correct; the inclination of the man to one or the other of these associations is mainly determined by his feelings; they do not rest to any great extent upon his judgment as to particular actions. When it comes to advocating this or that measure, — as, for instance, a protective tariff, or silver at 16 to 1, — the man usually, to the great advantage of good government, follows the lead of some public man for whose ability he has respect. He thinks that he is acting independently, but, in fact, he is doing what is in most cases a much better thing, — he is acting on expert advice. Thus it comes about that the decisions concerning the most important matters with which the state had to deal are in all important regards for the masses determined by a few hundred or a few thousand men to whom the people have learned to look for guidance. It is, therefore, to the quality of these leaders quite as much as to the reasoning of the greater number of the voters that we have to look for the safe conduct of the state.

Much as intelligence and education are to be desired, what is even more needed in the voter is moral rather than intellectual qualities; if he is patriotic, — desires the good of the commonwealth above his personal advantage, — if he has a fair judgment as to the ability and honesty of men, the country will be safe in his hands; it will certainly not go forward in the higher work of statesmanship as rapidly as it would if all the men on whom the state rests were able to understand just what they were about. Yet under the conditions which we can foresee, the management of the country has to be left to leaders, — in other words, in every democracy the spirit and quality of motives must come from the body of the people, while the details of action are carried out by those to whom they intrust their affairs.

On the whole, the safest ground for the citizen to take with reference to the question of universal suffrage seems to be that, if possible, the only qualifications should be those of education and honesty. All efforts to better the system should be directed to the schooling of the people, and especially towards awakening those qualities which make for patriotism.

The question of extending the suffrage to women on the same conditions on which it is held by men is now distinctly before our people. It has already been thus extended in some of the western states of this Union. There seem to be no good reasons, if the suffrage be regarded as a right, why women are not entitled to it as well as men. The question really is, however, whether the safest and most reasonable view is not that the vote is given to but a part of the citizens for the reason that the public good can better be attained in that way than by calling on all to render this service. As the most of the voters are men of families, the method used at present is in effect a system of household suffrage, so that each home commonly has a share in political affairs. Women are represented by their influence with the voters to whom they are related.

The main objection to allowing women to vote is that it would greatly increase the number of persons in our commonwealth who have to be educated in political matters. At present this body is exces-

UNIVERSAL SUFFRAGE

sively large, being about twenty million. To add another twenty million of persons who, from their necessarily secluded lives, are not well placed to obtain knowledge of political matters, will be to incur certain danger. Men gather their information on political matters from their contact with the outer world; it comes to them in their affairs; in their dealings with others there usually enters much of politics; their away-from-home life, — in a word, fits them to receive much political education to which women cannot well have access.

If it should come about that a majority of the women in this country very much desire to have the right to vote, and feel themselves oppressed by the denial of this right, it will probably be best to give them the franchise; and this for the reason that it is most undesirable, as before remarked, to have any considerable body of our people in a discontented state. A democracy is primarily to insure the happiness of people; if it fails to attain this end, it fails altogether.

One of the evils of universal suffrage — an evil which would doubtless be augmented by allowing women to vote — is that in ordinary elections the greater number of those who should go to the polls fail to do so; they cast their votes only on those rare occasions when there is some exciting matter up for discussion. People who vote in this way usually do the task with very little discretion. They act under excitement, which is the one thing the voter should not do. So far as he can, the patriotic citizen should endeavour to avoid this evil of neglect of his franchise by being himself faithful to the obligation, and by inciting others to a like sense of duty by the great trust. It is a question whether a continued neglect of this duty should not disqualify a man from voting; it is clear that those who care so little for the privilege to use it with regularity are not worthy of the trust which has been placed in their hands.

In considering the matter of voting, the citizen should see that the motive which guides the vote is the corner-stone of the system of government in which he lives. So long as men act honestly and patriotically in this part of the state work, though their action may lead to grave errors, the evils thus entailed will quickly be repaired. Thus, in the question concerning the change in our monetary system which was recently under debate and still is contended for by some people, if the majority should decide to make silver the basis of our business, and it should turn out that the consequences are highly injurious to the affairs of the country, the people, if their aim in making the change were patriotic, would quickly undo the action and return to the gold basis. The money loss from the mistake might be great, but the people would have had a lesson in government which might serve them well hereafter. If, on the other hand, the object of the masses is, as some believe (the writer is not among them), to defraud those who have loaned money, with the expectation that it would be paid back in a currency of equal value to that which was lent, the state would be in a bad way, for there would be need of a moral reform which it would be hard to bring about. We thus see that the well-intentioned blunders of patriotic people, due to ignorance, though they may be costly, are not, save when they lead to war, overwhelmingly so; they are usually retrieved very quickly, and the results are highly educative.

RELIGION AND THE STATE

The most noteworthy feature in this nation is an entire separation of matters concerning religion from the affairs of the federal and the local governments. The Constitution of the United States does not even mention the name of the Almighty. All documents of this nature in this country limit their mention of religion to statements that men shall be free to believe as they please, and to worship or not to worship as they may elect. In a few states a man is by law not allowed to give evidence before a court unless he has some religious belief; but this is a mere matter of administration, the ground for the action being doubt whether a man who does not believe in punishment for his sins after death will be bound by his oath to tell the truth.

The failure to recognise the Creator in our Constitution offends some people who do not know the history of this action. The fathers of our government lived in a time when the civilised people of the world were just escaping from many centuries of sore trials due to the union of church and state. In the two hundred years before the American Revolution many of the best of the English people were cruelly executed because of their religious belief. To depart from the state religion meant not only to become a heretic, but to commit treason. Even in the American colonies, though they were in good part founded to escape from this system of religious persecution which was made possible by the union of church and state, many were imprisoned because of their apostasy from the legally established church. The most prominent and important feature of our great charter, the Constitution, — one that separates it from all similar documents, — is that in it, for the first time, a nation assumed that government and religion were separate matters, and that neither should control the other. With this separation the establishment of democratic government effectively began, for the complete freedom of the man could not be obtained until it was impossible for any one to dictate his beliefs.

At this time there seems in this country little reason to fear a return to the ancient union of church and state. There remains, however, among

RELIGION AND THE STATE

some of our people an apprehension lest the Roman Catholic Church, a body which is supposed to hold to the old ideas concerning that union, should in some way contrive to obtain possession of the government and renew the ancient oppression. Against this supposition we may set the fact that since the foundation of this government Roman Catholics have constituted a considerable part of the population, and in no case have they proved less patriotic than those of other Christian faiths. Among the early settlers there were considerable bodies of folk who never adopted the Protestant belief. These people rendered distinguished service in the Revolutionary War. A large number of our best citizens are of the same persuasion; several of the famous generals who commanded Union armies during the Civil War were of this ancient faith. It is true that our nation is characteristically Protestant; it is probable, indeed, that the United States would not have originated among people of other belief; but there appears to be nothing in our system of government that makes it in any way difficult for those of the Roman Church to render it true and patriotic service.

It is urged by those who oppose the Roman Church that it holds to the doctrine that the authority of the Pope is supreme; that his commands are superior to those of any and all other persons. It is not easy for a Protestant to find out just what this means, but so far as the writer has been able to ascertain, it means that among the Roman Catholics in the matters of faith, as distinguished from matters of government, the Church is the supreme authority.

The only grave political dispute between the Protestants and Catholics concerns the management of the public schools. The older church desires that the children of its people receive religious instruction along with their general education. They therefore wish to have a portion of the public-school money set aside to pay, in part at least, the costs of such schools. The body of the Protestants object to this arrangement, for the reason that these schools should not be used for the propagation of any particular religious belief. If such a division were made it would inevitably weaken the system, which would doubtless be in turn still further endangered by like arrangements with other divisions of Christians. There is no reason to believe that any such separation can ever be established: our people are devoted to their system of public education and are not likely to allow changes which will weaken it.

But while some friction may naturally arise from this desire of the Catholics to make essential changes in our educational system, it is very desirable that it should not lead to any effort to exclude members of this body of Christians from a full share in our national life. Any such action would be in effect a reintroduction by the Protestants of that system

RELIGION AND THE STATE

of religious persecution from which our forefathers, who knew its evils so well, undertook to protect us by the separation of church and state. Granting that there may be a certain element of danger to our institutions from the claims and endeavours of a church which is managed from abroad, this is no reason why we should seek the evident dangers which would come from introducing once again religious tests in our political system.

If at any time it should appear that the followers of a church were undertaking to get possession of our government, or any part of it, we may be sure that the patriotism of our people would at once and effectively deal with those misguided people by the simple and effectual method of outvoting them. In the mean time each citizen will do best to proceed on the assumption that his comrades of the state, upheld by their religious belief, sincerely desire to maintain it in its integrity, and that anything they may endeavour to accomplish is not meant to injure the commonwealth. To hold an attitude of suspicion and hostility to a body of people who have never failed to support our government is to bring back into our society something of the intolerance which for so many centuries was the curse of mankind.

From the point of view of the citizen, it is in the highest measure desirable that Christianity should prosper and that it should profoundly affect the conduct of every person in the state. Experience shows that the soundness of a government such as our own depends upon the existence of religious motives among the people. It is clearly the main source of patriotism, for it leads to those relations between men, and to that sense of duty, which are the foundations of true democracy. It is at the same time clear that churches must be left to do their work in their own way without any aid from or control of the government; they need freedom for their life as much as do the people of the commonwealth for their political existence.

THE NEGRO QUESTION

Among the most serious of the many questions which American citizens have to face is that which arises from the fact that a large part of our people are Africans of a race very unlike our own, whose ancestors were brought here as slaves. At present these strangers, for such they still are for all their long residence in this land, number about one-seventh of the whole population; in the extreme southern states of this Union they are nearly half as numerous as those of European parentage. They are a wholesome people, and their gain in numbers appears to be quite as great as that of the white population. They are by nature laborious, and to their toil we owe the greater part of the agriculture of ten states, and somewhere near one-sixth of all the tillage of this country.

NEGRO QUESTION

For many years there was the fallacious hope that these negroes would in some way disappear; by returning to Africa as colonists or by fading away before the competition of the whites in the manner of other primitive races, or through the effects of the northern climate which was supposed to be deadly to all tropical folk. Experience shows that these blacks are unwilling to return to the land whence our forefathers brought them. We could not afford to compel them to go there, for we could not spare their services. To send them forth against their will would be an iniquity which no civilised people could perpetuate. They are to abide in this commonwealth; to help it or to harm it as the whites, who are still the masters of their destiny, may in large part determine. It is therefore the duty of every true citizen to see what should be done to help this people, so that they may be set upon the way of advancement to the dignity of citizenship.

To understand the negro question in its relations to our society and government we need to look over the history of the coming of the Africans to the New World and the place they have held since their advent. This may be briefly stated as follows: When the first colonists settled in this country near three hundred years ago, they at once found themselves in grave need of labourers. They were themselves few in number and had to win a wilderness to their needs. At that time the mother country was still scantily peopled; its population being less than the fourth part of what it is at present. It had recently been lessened by a succession of pestilences. If these feeble colonies were to maintain themselves, they had to find access to some class of labourers. Efforts were made to obtain such a supply by sentencing English minor criminals to be sold for a period for service in America, but these folk proved of little value to those who bought their time. There was also much effort to induce the Indians to work for wages or to force the prisoners of this race taken in war to labour, but neither reward nor punishment had ever served to make an effective labourer of the red man. He will work but little for himself, and if forced to do so for another, he quickly dies. At this stage of the difficulty it was discovered, at first by the Spaniards, who began the colonisation of America nearly a century before the English, that at the price of a few strings of beads or a gallon of rum a man could be bought in Africa who was fairly docile and an excellent, enduring labourer. The average cost of purchasing these people of their chief or masters, and of transporting them to the American coast, was but a few dollars, — scarcely more than the expense of bringing cattle across the sea. As soon as this African source of labour became well known, it was availed of in a very rapid manner; a considerable fleet of slavers became engaged in the business, so that for more than a hundred years

NEGRO QUESTION

there was a plentiful supply of slaves in the American markets.

In considering the moral as well as the economic side of the slave trade, the man of to-day must take care not to judge of it as he would if the business were done in his own time. All our ideas as to the evils of this institution when the sufferers are of an alien and lowly race are very modern, — hardly more than a century old. They are a part of the later gains in the field of morals. To our ancestors of the seventeenth century the process of enslaving savages was about as much a matter of course as the capturing of wild beasts. It is well also to note that these enslaved negroes were not debased by the change from their native countries to America. On the contrary, they gained in opportunities of life, for they came into contact with a superior race; they were thus trained out of barbarism and into a Christian civilisation. So that they and their descendants had a chance of rising to a plane of life which has never come and most likely never will come to others of their kind. Moreover, the help which the negroes gave as labourers in the colonies south of the Hudson, and in a less degree to the more northern settlements as well, was of the utmost value to the development of the English power on this continent. There is, indeed, grave doubt whether our people could have maintained their place against the Indians, the French, and the Spaniards without the good help they had from these gentle and laborious folk from Africa. The political conditions of the time were such that they needed quickly to become strong, and the needed strength could not have been won by their own hands. Thus while we of to-day see that there was an immoral quality in the slave trade, it for a time proved exceedingly helpful to a good cause.

After the Revolutionary War, slavery, never having had much importance in the region north of Maryland, gradually became restricted to what is called the South, being maintained in five of the thirteen original states and in time extended to eight others organised after the federal government was founded, so that the slaveholding section of this country became considerably larger than the original colonies. As a result of much controversy, slaveholding was restricted to that part of the United States where tobacco or cotton was the staple product of agriculture, — crops which can be advantageously reared on large plantations and for which slave labour is well suited. Although white men can work in the fertile lowlands of the South, the summers are so long and hot that the region must be regarded as near the southern limit to which our race can go. It is doubtful if this region could have been developed if it had depended on white labour, or if it could now go forward with a people derived from the stocks of northern Europe. The negroes have given us the share of success it has attained, and on their labour its further progress clearly depends.

NEGRO QUESTION

The system of slavery in this country in the more than two centuries during which it existed was, on the whole, as little iniquitous as an institution of its essentially evil nature could well be. The masters were generally merciful. Their close relations with their servants broke down the instinctive dislike which is so effective a bar for sympathy where white men are casually brought in contact with black people. In fact, in the best condition of the institution the slave had a chance to form good, human, affectionate relations with our race such as freedom generally denies him. Where he was a household servant or a labourer on a small plantation looked after by his master, he generally had a precious opportunity such as has never been given to any other primitive man, to be rid of savagery and to learn the most important lessons of a Christian civilisation. That he has been lifted in less than six generations to where we now find him, to an average station that no savages have ever acquired, is due to the instruction which was forced upon him as a slave, and could not have come to him under other conditions.

Good as slavery was as a school for the negro, it held in it the foundations of great evils, at first for the whites and in time for the blacks as well. The system is one that is evidently impossible in a democracy which rests absolutely on the freedom of the men in its commonwealth. A slave-owner, though he be of the highest type and may have a certain nobility, cannot be a democrat, — he must be an aristocrat in spirit; thus slavery inevitably separated the whites of the South from their brethren of the North by all the differences that a social system can create. Moreover, with the tendency to massed industries which we see so clearly in this day, but which began to be operative near a century ago, slavery, at first and for long of the household and farm type, tended more and more to the methods of large plantations where the blacks were gathered by hundreds or even thousands to be driven to their work by taskmasters and ruled by the commonly despicable hired overseers. So rapid had been this change in the period from about 1820 to 1860 that the educational value of slavery to the black was in good part lost and the effect on the owners and administrators of those great estates far more evil than before.

So far as the historic record shows, the political contest between the north and the south began with the question as to the extension of slavery to the new states of the region west of the Mississippi River, which were to be carved out of the national domain acquired by the purchase of Louisiana from France in 1803. The Civil War began with the election of Lincoln as president, the Southerners claiming that as they could not have protection under the federal Constitution they would withdraw from the Union. It is not difficult to see that the reason assigned for secession, though honestly advanced, was not the true foundation for that action. This is to be sought in the state of mind developed by the system of slavery which had parted the southern ruling class from the men of the North. What the secessionists instinctively strove for was a formal separation from the democratic motive which still controlled the larger part of the country. The result of the war was to break down what had become the most characteristic aristocracy of modern times, and to give a chance for the democratic spirit which had long been developed in the North to control the whole country.

It is well that we should look upon the wonderful incidents of the Civil War without the prejudices which moved the contestants on either side; that we should see in it, as historians will in time come to see, the actions of men as they are controlled by their institutions, even when they have no idea that they are thus controlled. The writer, a native of a slave-holding state, was by circumstances near to the men of both North and South. He knows that they were alike moved by the sincerest patriotism, yet neither recognised that the controversies of the moment concerned were those diverse ideals of government for which our race is ever willing to battle. The southern people honestly believed that they were not fighting for slavery, but for a rather shadowy thing called state rights; the northern at first that they were not in arms to free the slaves, but to save the Federal Union, yet it is clear that the combat was between two ideals of government: the ancient aristocratic ideal, which had been restored in this country by the system of slavery, and that of democracy of the American type.

The results of the Civil War were twofold: firstly, it affirmed the democratic character of this nation; secondly, it made an end of slavery on this continent, and we may say throughout the civilised world, — for such remnants of the institution as existed elsewhere were soon swept away by the great movement which our action brought about. The consequences of the extension of the democratic motive to the whole of this country have been very great. At first it is true they were destructive, for it brought about a great change in southern society. In the end it will doubtless be helpful to the whole of the United States.

Whoever looks over the history of the contest that led to the overthrow of slavery, with some sense of the history of men, will see how their actions are shaped by the institutions which they have inherited. He will behold in slavery an evil, though at first profitable, — a system of human relations which in time came to warp near half our people from their true ideals, destroying the precious ideal of human liberty and the love of the government on which the preservation of that liberty depends. It will be clear to him that if the Confederacy had been established the result would have been the development on this continent of two strong, consolidated nations, each armed against the other and animated by hatreds that would have led to endless war. State rights, the nominal object of the southern contention, would have vanished before the need of consolidated power. The military state of mind, such as debases the peoples of continental Europe, would have replaced the peaceful motive which belongs of right to our union of commonwealths. The considerate observer will further see, what our countrymen have admirably recognised, that the inevitable war fitly ended with the surrender of the Confederates; that there was left no question as to the good faith of the men of both sides who by ill fortune had been driven to take part in the great debate which determined the future of this land.

The only part of the ancient trouble that survives the Civil War is the negro element of our population. There can be no question as to the seriousness of the trouble which the presence of these people entails on us. As before noted, they were when they came to us as completely foreign to the purposes of our society and government as were the aborigines of this country. They were commonly and in most regards of much lower quality than the American Indian. Their training as slaves developed their innate fitness for toiling and forced them to conform to our habits of life; it had moreover taught them to use our language in an effective manner. It had, however, taught them nothing in the way of that self-reliance which is the foundation of the citizen's value; nor anything of the sense of property on which success in free life so intimately depends.

This huge mass of undeveloped folk, greater in number than the inhabitants of England when the American colonies were founded, more numerous than the population of the Federal Union when it was formed, were by the issue of the war made nominally free and in a like nominal way given the right to share in the government of the country. It is difficult to see, in the then state of the public mind, what else could have been done with the blacks; but this sudden and totally unprepared change was a great injustice to them. They were forced at once to undertake a work for which their masters, an abler folk, trained by centuries of citizenly experience, are not yet completely fitted. The most hopeful feature of the situation is that the blacks have not made far worse use of these dangerous gifts of freedom and the franchise than they have done. Except for a few months of disturbance, with scarce a trace of violence, immediately following the end of the war, the greater part of this people have held to their tasks. They are now even as laborious as they were when slaves, as is well shown by the fact that the crops they till yield quite as much to each negro employed in their tillage as in the time of their slavery.

NEGRO QUESTION

Where they have not been deprived of the right to vote by state laws, they have, in the South at least, generally ceased to make use of that right, in which the mass of them have little or no citizenly interest.

If the only question concerning the negro's place with us were that of willingness to work and submission to the laws, there would be no great reason for apprehension as to their future. They could be left to lie where they now are, at the bottom of our society, where, indeed, lie a large part of our foreign-born nominal citizens. It is, however, evident that if they are thus left they will in time form a peasant class about as effectively slaves as of old. Their presence will discredit hand labour in the eyes of the poorer whites. We shall have in a slightly changed form the same problem that the war for a time swept away. It may be that this result is inevitable; it certainly is so unless the blacks, or considerable part of them, can be lifted to the plane of true citizenship. That this good end may, by due effort, be attained is indicated by the facts set forth below.

The first point to note in considering the future of the negro and the ways in which he may be advanced, is that admirable endurance to toil, which gave him his great value as a slave. A capacity for labour is seldom found among savages. More than any other part of man it shows a capacity for civilisation, for by it alone all the material basis of advancement can be won. Next in order of value is the fact that this African people is not of one stock, but an admixture of very diverse races. There is, indeed, in these Africans, under the effective mark of a common colour and character of hair, a far greater variety of stocks than are blended in our white population. Such differences in quality were naturally to a great extent hidden during slavery, which tends to keep a subjected folk in a uniform condition; they have had no chance to develop their capacities. Those who have had the chance and the desire to study our American negroes, have learned something of their wide differences of ability and character; how, while a large number of them, perhaps over one-third, are still in mind a very lowly people with scant intelligence and rude passions, the greater part of the folk are fairly quick-witted, and many have a true manliness that we may hope to see ripen into a high grade citizenly quality. Sometimes, though rarely, we find a man of capacity fit to be compared with that of the abler whites. It is likely that these differences are due to the exceeding variety of the stock whence the ancestors of these people came: the range being from the lowly, rather timid, savage of the Guinea coast, from which the lowliest seem to have been derived, to the brave and intelligent Zulus of the southern part of Africa and the vigorous, manly Basutos of the regions about the upper waters of the Nile.

It is in the evidently great variety of the negroes

NEGRO QUESTION

that we find the best chance of dealing with the problem of fitting them to our commonwealth; for from this range of nature we may hope to develop men who will fit well in various stations, and in time to bring a large part of the people above the peasant grade. The first need is to provide as well as we can for their training in the simpler arts, so that they may be made good carpenters, masons, metal-workers, etc. It was by this education of the trades that our own people won the most important of their schooling and in the course of centuries gained their development. It must be on this same slow, hard road, and not to any extent by a literary education, that the negro is to find his way to the full station of the citizen. Of late, after a generation of blundering, our people, the blacks, as well as the whites, under the leadership of General Armstrong and Booker Washington, have come to see the need and value of training for the various higher industries, and are providing the means of giving it to the negro youth of both sexes.

It will be a difficult task to obtain the means for the training which Mr. Washington seeks to give his people. The task has to be done in states which are still poor from the losses of the war, and where the whites cannot afford like opportunities for their own children. No community in the world has as yet been able to establish such a system of industrial education. Yet, as it appears to provide the only way of escape from the immediate dangers of the situation, it should have the support of every earnest citizen.

The obstacle which is likely to prove the most permanent bar to the complete reconciliation of the negro to our American commonwealth, is the prejudice of race the whites feel to peoples very unlike themselves. As before remarked, this prejudice is a natural animal motive, such as causes dogs to be at perpetual enmity with their kinsmen, the foxes or the wolves. It has been of some service to mankind in the lower stages of development, as it has led tribes to keep to themselves and to take a pride in their good qualities. It has served well in limiting those mixtures of the blood of diverse races of men which commonly give rise to " half-breed " offspring. But when two diverse races are associated as are the blacks and whites in this country, the effect of this prejudice is in many regards most unhappy. It prevents that exchange of sympathies and understanding on which the success of the society intimately depends. No truly democratic commonwealth is possible where the folk are divided into two bodies, sharply and permanently separated from each other. Differences of ranks based on education or wealth may exist without serious consequences, for they are not permanent: they rest on values that may be gained or lost. Thus it comes about that the English aristocracy is tolerated and even admired in a society that is, in most regards, essentially democratic; the reason being that an untitled youth of ability may, if he be fortunate, find his way into it. But a caste system, where the division rests upon abiding dislikes, would destroy our existing society more completely than could any tyrant.

It thus appears that the part of the helpful citizen in dealing with the negro problem may well be found in an effort to advance the education of that people in ways that will serve to fit them for the simpler yet honourable positions of trained workmen, leaving the ordinary means of the higher education open to the abler youth, as they should be to all who are fit for such schooling. At the same time he should protest against that dislike of the negroes as a race, which all Americans, except those who have been brought into intimate relations with them in their youth, appear to feel. That this prejudice, though strong, is not ineradicable, is shown by the close, sympathetic relations which were often developed between the masters and servants in the old days of slavery, and which were the redeeming features of that evil. We should make our people see that this blind dislike of any man is more than unworthy of them; it is, in fact, disgraceful that, large-minded folk as they in general are, they should be influenced by a motive that is essentially brutal, — one from which the cultivated peoples of the Old World have long ago escaped.

It should be understood that it is not necessary that the social recognition of the negroes should go so far as to insure their admission to the homes of the whites on the same basis as determines the entrance of persons of our own race. It is, indeed, very undesirable that the two peoples should ever be linked by marriage, for the offsprings of such marriages are almost always weak and short-lived. Whenever they have formed a mixed race, it has proved much less good than either of the parent stocks. We thus have to accept this limitation on the intercourse, yet it is one that need not bear hardly on either race, for it is for the best interests of both. It is common enough in our best and most democratic communities for a part of the families to dwell quite apart from the others without in any way contemning those whom they would not for various reasons welcome to their homes. So much of caste distinction is necessary in any developed society, yet these limitations on intercourse need not seriously lessen the sympathy which men need have with one another in the social life that is beyond the household, — in matters of public policy and utility, wherein lies the life of the commonwealth. What is imperatively wanted is that the negroes be admitted there and that their welcome be in the measure of their citizenly quality, undiminished by any reference to their race.

It is not to be denied that the task of developing

the latent powers, which, in the opinion of the writer, are far greater than is generally believed, is very serious. Nothing like it has ever before been undertaken. It may before completed demand for its accomplishment something like as large a share of the national wealth as was expended by the federal government during the Civil War. It means a certain amount of technical education of a very great number of the children of ten million people, say to not less than one hundred thousand for years to come. As it is not likely that the white people will allow schools of this quality to exist for negroes alone, it may mean that a like education will have to be opened to both races, — a result certainly not to be deplored. Yet this cost need not affright us, for we may be sure that this, like all other well-directed education, will be a very good investment of public money, for it will bear fruit in money as well as other values. Every black man otherwise to be a mere plodding labourer, who by such training is lifted to the grade of a skilled artisan, will have his value to the state increased several fold. His annual earnings as a "field hand" will not exceed one hundred and fifty dollars; as a skilled blacksmith, carpenter, or machinist, they should be at least four hundred dollars; and in something like this measure his value will be advanced by his training.

Good as the financial result of training the negroes as artisans is likely to be, that to be had from the improvement of their station is yet better. So long as these folk lie at the bottom of our economic system and are reckoned as mere labourers, who accumulate no property and gain none of the station which property gives, the contempt for their lowliness will add to that which comes to them on account of their race. As soon, however, as they begin to gain wealth and have a place in the higher grades of employment, they will have a certainty of recognition as citizens. A few score negroes who had acquired fortunes in honest industry would go far towards breaking down the barriers that now debar their people from a fair chance of becoming citizens of high grade.

CHAPTER XII

FOREIGN POSSESSIONS

NEXT in importance to the great problem of dealing with the negroes of this country is that brought about by the conquests of the Spanish War, — what may be termed the question of foreign possessions, not colonies, as they are generally misnamed, but conquests of land and peoples in regions remote from our country. This question, like many another our people have had to face, has at once a moral and an economic side. It concerns at once the matter of right doing and of profit to the material interests of the commonwealth.

We should at first note that the question is not of acquiring new territory for national use, that we have done many times before, by buying it from Spain and France, or the Indians, nor even of winning such territory by force of arms, that we did in the Mexican War, with no credit to our national honour, but without more shame than commonly lies in the way of conquests. The question is whether we should definitely enter on the ancient way followed by other countries, of subduing foreign peoples for our profit, — a way which this nation deliberately avoided in the first century of its history. Although we have entered on this way, and have forcibly taken possession of Porto Rico and of the Philippines, the action was suddenly taken, without any reference of it, by an election, to the judgment of the citizens of the republic. Therefore, the action is to be regarded as tentative, and the policy it represents as one still to be determined by debate.

In debating with himself and others the question whether this nation should hold subjugated countries without reference to the will of their peoples, the true citizen will turn first to the matter of right and wrong involved in the action. He will remember that he holds his citizenship in a commonwealth that claimed and won its place among states by contending for certain plain rights of man, not rights that were peculiarly their own, but the common property of all men. It will not be amiss for him to read again the Declaration of Independence, which is in many ways the noblest of the many "bills of right" by which men of our race, from Runnymede to Philadelphia, have set forth their idea of what liberty means. If he reads this part of the lesson as the writer does, he cannot escape the conclusion that to conquer and hold any people on any pretence whatever is to deny the very basis of our government, and to turn against the motives that have guided our commonwealth to all the moral dignity and greatness it has won.

FOREIGN POSSESSIONS

Although it seems to be impossible to reconcile the conquest of foreign countries and their subjugation to our purposes with the Declaration of Independence, or the rules which have piloted our nation for more than a century, it may be urged, and this with some fair show of reason, that we have outlived the early conditions of our national life, and are now by circumstances driven to do as others do in the rude scramble for national success; that the question before us is not to be decided by what our ancestors said or did, but by the needs of our time.

It may be granted that there come times in the history of a people when they have to turn their backs upon their past, when they may have to abandon their ancient ideals of life and duty for new motives which changes in conditions force them to adopt. It may further be granted that it is a part of patriotism to make such changes boldly, and with a full understanding that men cannot do their duty by their generation if they give themselves to a blind worship of what other generations have done. Our English ancestors in their rebellion against the Stuart kings, our colonies in the Revolution of 1776, did just this; they were right, and those who held to ancient traditions of loyalty were wrong. The question is under what circumstances a people are justified in putting aside the principles which the experience of their commonwealth has proved to be honest and safe rules of previous action, to adopt new ways of dealing with their fellow-men. Clearly the reasons for the change need be weighty; they should, indeed, be in their nature compelling. They must concern the safety of the state, the chance of its people to win their bread, or to do their just part by their fellow-men.

As regards the conduct of a state in those crises where there is a temptation to enter on a new mode of life that contradicts its accepted bases of action, we may compare it with that of an individual man who has lived and prospered by shaping his deeds on certain rules which have always seemed to him right. There comes a crisis in his affairs when he sees the way to profit by giving up his high ideals for those he has heretofore considered as base. If he gives way to the temptation, we judge him degraded. If he robs his neighbours to help his business, we send him to the penitentiary; or if he does the wrong on so large a scale that the law cannot check him, we judge him a tyrant to be overcome by arms. Yet when we look at the matter critically, we see that the acts of a state are subject to the judgments which fit the people as a whole quite as closely as they fit any individual citizen. It is, indeed, to this way of looking at the responsibility of the individual citizen for what the state does or leaves undone that we owe the development of our democracy,—the efficient patriotism that makes it valuable. Of old, there was a notion that a state

FOREIGN POSSESSIONS

was something else than an association of people where each had all the responsibility of a sovereign. It was supposed to be established by heaven through the divine right given to its rulers, so that its citizens, or rather subjects, had no other duty than to submit to their sacred rule. To get rid of this idea as to the relation of the state to those who dwell in it has cost the lives of a multitude of men whom we properly regard as our heroes; whose memories we keep sacred, and on whom we call for help in trouble; we bless them for the reason that they made us free to judge the actions of the state as our own. It is from considerations such as these that we should approach the question as to the wisdom and justice of establishing by conquest a system of foreign possessions.

In considering the right and policy of gaining control of foreign lands and peoples by war, it will be well first to note the arguments for so doing. These, in brief, are as follows: In the first place, it is maintained that the United States has now come to a stage of development, commercial and industrial, where it imperatively needs to have a fair share in the markets of the world, and that as the great states of Europe are rapidly grasping the lands of all peoples who are not strong enough to maintain their independence, we should do our share of the grabbing, lest we soon find that our trade is narrowed by the tariffs of those states. This argument has a certain brutal force, but, tested by the right of an individual to despoil his neighbour for his own profit, it is seen to have a distinct criminal quality. Moreover, if there were no objections to the scheme from a moral point of view, there would remain others very serious from that of policy. It is a well-known fact that none of the newly won possessions of France or Germany have begun to pay their costs to those governments; they are all maintained at a very serious loss of money and the lives of the garrisons needed to hold them in subjection. Probably the only really profitable foreign possession held by a European power is Java, which yields a large return to the Dutch government, for the reason that it is exceptionally fruitful, and its people are forced to labour practically as slaves.

There is another argument akin to that just considered, which is to the effect that we need these so-called colonies in order that the youth of our commonwealth may have a wider chance to win fortune and station than our country can afford them. The example of England is pointed to as showing how these holdings serve to give her youth a chance to rise. Whatever may be the need of outside possessions in the case of a small country like Great Britain, such need clearly does not exist with us. It is our good fortune that our home place is so large that our children do not need to seek their chance in life in foreign parts; moreover, except as regards a relatively few government offices, the chance of an American in the British colonies is just as good as those of a subject of its crown. Granting that this need is great, the question is whether we should satisfy it by taking what does not belong to us, or, after the manner of honest men, let the need go unsatisfied.

Probably the strongest argument for foreign possessions is that by holding them we may be able in time greatly to benefit their peoples. Although, as experience, that of our own and all other nations, clearly shows, we must begin such benefaction with war, it is held that we may, after due subjugation, establish in those conquered lands schools, savings banks, legislatures, manhood, suffrage, and the other institutions we have proved good with us; so, in time, we may lift them to our own plane of liberty. It is said that in the administration of these foreign possessions we should find reward for the temporary ills of war, pestilence, famine, and enduring hatreds that all armed conquests entail. It is a fine dream, this fancy of far-away lands mercifully compelled to give over their ancient rule and to submit themselves to that of a great free commonwealth which desires only their good. Those who know something of conquests since the beginnings of history know that they are rarely undertaken for mere plunder, but most commonly for some seeming lofty purpose, — to spread the gospel of peace; to thwart the desires of some base exploiter of the earth; or to help an unhappy people to better ways of living.

It is here with the many men of the state as it is with the individual man, — stealing is rarely mere barefaced stealing to the thief; it is rather a process of appropriation by which the goods in question may be made to yield a larger return in the way of true values in the hands of the new holder.

If we look a moment at the matter of the benefits we may give to conquered aliens, we see yet other and very strong reasons why our benevolent purpose cannot be attained; for we shall see that a system of government and social institutions which serves well the people who in the course of centuries have developed them may prove entirely unsuited to a folk of another history. We see this near at hand when we consider the fate of the Indians in this country. It is the custom absolutely to condemn the conduct of our folk towards the people they found in this land. There is, it is true, much in that conduct that is reprehensible, but when we take the whole history of these relations, we see that the root of the trouble lay in the utter incapacity of the Indian to fit himself to our institutions. At the outset there were many and faithful efforts to bring him into our social system; many schools, including Harvard College, in part or in whole, were founded for his education, and many devoted men gave their lives to the vain effort to domesticate the wild man under our English roof. It was not until the red man proved unalterably wild that the alternative process of extermination began. To our forefathers the obdurate wildness of the Indian was an evidence of original ineradicable sin that justified them in slaying him. To our better knowledge it is clear that the Indian, by his nature and history, was debarred from living under our institutions; good as they were to us, they were death to him. He had his fitting institutions as old and as elaborated as our own; they came forth from his nature, and were thus suited to his needs as no others could be.

A larger and more telling instance of the difficulty encountered in forcing alien peoples prosperously in the ways that we tread is found in our experience with the Africans, who have been near two hundred years with us. Although they form but a small minority of our population, and have been for generations in close contact with our society, the gravest problem our country has to face is as to the means by which they may be brought into the state of American citizens. As elsewhere noted, the task is one likely to tax our resources of money and devotion to public good to the uttermost. Yet these people are here with us and not beyond the seas. They speak our language, share our religion, and are pathetically anxious to be like ourselves; there were, indeed, never more willing pupils of a state than they are, but the result of the mutual endeavour for a common citizenship remains uncertain.

Some further light is thrown on the probable results of an effort to bring the folk of our foreign possessions by the experience of other countries. France and Spain long held the island that is now occupied by the so-called republics of Hayti and San Domingo. The negroes there were apparently as civilisable as those of the United States; at the time of their revolt from European control their state of culture gave promise of a fair future. The heroic Toussaint L'Ouverture and many of his followers appeared to indicate a safe quality in the people. Yet since their emancipation these people have steadily gone downward, and are now, from all accounts, about where they were when they were brought from Africa. St. John, for twenty-five years the British minister to Hayti, asserts that in some parts of that country the people have reverted to cannibalism, connecting the practice with their revered heathen rites, and that he has known members of the government to take part in this degradation. It is fair to say that these grave charges have been denied by several honest though apparently less competent observers, but the fact remains that an evidently truthful man of high position and long experience in the country thus judged its folk.

Looking the world over, we fail to discover a clear instance in which subjugated peoples of alien races have been led to look up to their conquerors, to adopt their institutions, and regard them as their friends, and few in which their armed masters have been able to do them any real service. The most notable of those exceptions, those often adduced in this argument, are in their nature exceptional, — that of the British rule in India, where the strong nation managed to make an end to wars and oppressions among the various states of the peninsula, and thus gave the people a better chance in life; and that where a like rule in Egypt has dispersed an ancient tyranny that ground the people to the earth. In such instances a folk may welcome a new and better tyrant, but so far as we can see they never adopt his methods of thought and action, however great the inducement to do so may be, and this for the simple yet excellent reason that men cannot change their natures at their will.

The facts seem to make it clear that there is no possibility that we may bring the people of the Philippines, or other like folk we may conquer or purchase, into even a useful semblance of American citizens; that at best we can subdue them and keep them subjected at great cost; we can force on them a rule they dislike and bring them to conform to certain usages they detest; we can more or less effectively break up the social and political conditions which they have shaped for themselves, and which, however imperfect, fit them better than our own, but we cannot expect to bring them to our ways. To keep them at all will demand a greater annual expenditure than would apparently be required to train all our youths, both black and white, who need such training in the various artisan crafts. It is reckoned by expert military men that the permanent garrison of those islands would have to be at least ten thousand soldiers. The cost of this force, including its transportation, etc., will probably be about twenty million dollars per annum, and this without reckoning the value of the men who die prematurely because of their exposure to a tropical climate. We may fairly reckon this added death rate at an average of not less than thirty per thousand each year, and the money value of these lost men at five thousand dollars each. In the best possible conditions of commerce with the Philippines it is improbable that our people win back in trade as much as one-tenth of this vast expenditure.

Some of those who contend for the change of our policy that may give us permanent control of foreign lands, speak as if they look forward to a time when these territories will become the seat of true colonies of our people, offshoots of our national life, such as were the English colonies in America in the old days, or as Canada and Australia are now. They forget that all the lands available for such settlement outside of the tropics are now possessed by strong peoples, that there remain only the tropical countries, so defenceless that they may be easily obtained. They are defenceless because the native government of the tropics is always weak. Now there is overwhelming evidence that the regions within the tropics — all those, indeed, which lie at less distances than thirty degrees of latitude from the equator — are, except in their mountainous parts, unfit to be the seat of colonies of our northern folk. All the northern European people who have tried to establish themselves in these permanently hot regions have proved that even when the original settlers survive the trials of the climate their children are weak, and in a few generations the race becomes distinctly enfeebled; where it survives, it does so by becoming mixed with the native blood. Even the southern Spanish from their semi-tropical country become evidently lowered in quality if they remain for generations near the sea-level in the equatorial realm. It is evident that the men of our race are not fit for any land where the palms flourish; they do well only where snow rests on their housetops for a part of the year.

If, after considering the question of foreign possessions, the citizen determines that this country should go forward on the path upon which we were set by the events of the Spanish War, that we should follow the example of other states and bring under our rule peoples who do not desire to be ruled by us, we may have the consolation of knowing that the change in policy will not bring about any sudden or marked change in the conditions of our nation. There may, indeed, for a time be a certain gain in our self-esteem, from the sense that we are visibly a great power, with our " drum-beat heard around the world." As a man may outwardly prosper, though by his actions he has given the lie to his true purposes, so may a nation; but the degradation inevitably tells on the man or upon the concourse of them that makes a nation. As before remarked, a despotic government can do base deeds without harming the moral state of its subjects, for the reason that they have no power to determine whether such deeds are to be done or no; but in a democracy, because every man has a share in the action of the state, the shame is his to share. If he is overborne by a majority, he may clear his conscience by a vigorous protest; yet, as in a family, he cannot thereby quit himself of the disgrace that has been brought upon his house.

If it be asked, as it often is, how we are to be rid of our new possessions which came to us through the Spanish War, it may be answered that the process is easy, that we have already gone far in the task in bringing the Philippine Islands to the state of order in which they will be able to start governments of their own. That they are fit for this task of self-government is plain enough, for they have much patriotism and not a little capacity for organisation, as the trouble they have given us shows. When they are organised as a state, we should withdraw, keeping at most a protectorate over the country in order that it may not be assailed by other powers. But, say the advocates of our new policy, these people, with their seven or seventy different tribes, will fly at one another's throats, so our withdrawal will mean civil war. This is, indeed, very likely; but because a people may decide their differences in this brutal manner is no reason why we should hold them in subjection. Out of their strife there is likely to come some system of government that fits their need and desires far better than any we impose upon them. There can be no doubt that, if given the chance to be free, nearly all of our new subjects would choose freedom, were the risks many times as great as those they face.

There is only one basis on which the subjugation of foreign peoples can be defended on grounds that have any tincture of moral quality. This is by holding that their present state as subjects is only temporary, — is, in effect, an apprenticeship to their full dignity as citizens. In our republic, on this ground it might be urged that these primitive folk are in effect children whom we may coerce in order that they may come to a sound maturity. This argument is specious, for we know that we are, in fact, dealing with men, and no reasonable person expects to make these peoples full sharers with ourselves in the government of this nation. To bring a multitude of such folk from the ends of the earth into our federal legislatures would entail the swift ruin of our commonwealth. It is clear that if held under our rule, they must be held as subjects in conditions substantially like those under which we hold our Indians, with no expectation that they can ever rise to the dignity of free citizens. Our experience with this kind of rule in a century of relations with our subjected red men should make us most unwilling to go further in such experiments.

So far as the writer can find, there has been but one instance in which a primitive folk has been brought voluntarily to adopt the usages of our race and to a fair semblance of our motives. This exceptional case is that of the Polynesians, especially those of the Sandwich Islands. Here the missionaries, by persuasion alone, have accomplished a wonderful change in the manners of the originally gentle savages. They have, in effect, reduced them to civilisation. It is an unhappy fact that the Sandwich Islanders, once prosperous, have become greatly shrunken in the civilising process, and that the remnant appears to be in a way to disappear before the end of this century. This experiment, like all the others of a ruder sort, seems to indicate that primitive peoples cannot endure the conditions that suit the cultivated races; that civilisation, with its complexities, is not for them; they are, like the

FOREIGN POSSESSIONS

bison and the Indian, essentially untamable. They find what we call freedom a fatal slavery; the only good we can do them is to leave them politically alone. Such instances are but extreme examples of the general truth that each race and kind of man is so far peculiar that it cannot profitably have its government shaped by any other race, however strong and well-meaning that race may be.

Although it is the privilege and duty of the American citizen to decide this large question as such questions have not been decided by other peoples, on the basis of right-doing, it is not amiss that they look to the eventual results which may be expected, on the one hand, from adhering to our ancient democratic policy of having only free men in a free state, and on the other from the new project of holding foreign people as subjects. Let us essay this reckoning as to the probable future of our commonwealth in these diverse conditions. If we hold to the old well-tried method, it is easy to foresee that by the end of this century the territory of the United States, excluding the new-won islands, may have a population of about three hundred millions. Except so far as the quality of this folk may become debased by immigration of the lower grade people from southern and eastern Europe, or from our failure to lift the negroes, this folk should be in character superior to any other. We have a rich soil and a great body of mineral resources from which wealth may be earned. Our strength and separation from the contentions of other nations should keep us clear of impoverishing wars, and make us free to devote a larger share of our earnings to education and other means of advancement than any other people. All that Providence has given us may thus be profitably devoted to helping ourselves. We may thus expect that our children will see this nation strong, peaceful, and dominating the world for peace; a state that holds to the ideals of humanity, as does an honest man, which shall be a realm that in all its motives and actions helps to right living.

On the other hand, let us suppose we go forward in the way of imperialism. So doing, we shall doubtless have to be much engaged in war. We shall find our own Boers, Afghans, Ashantees, and other odds and ends of people who prefer freedom to the rule we would force on them. Now and then we shall have to fight one or another of the strong states of the Old World who are engaged in like marauding. Each new province will need its garrison; to the ten thousand required in the Philippines and other thousands in the Sandwich Islands, Porto Rico, etc., already in numbers near to twice the total of our army before the Spanish War, there will have to be added new hosts with each addition of subjugated territory. Then there will be need of a vast system of fortifications to make these possessions safe in time of war

FOREIGN POSSESSIONS

with other nations, and a fleet strong enough to enable us to cope with any one of them, or with any probable combination of two or more in alliance against us. This clearly means that we shall become a military nation; that we shall waste the strength which, husbanded by fairly enduring peace, has enabled us to spend on wages, education, and other means of bettering the state of men, in an effort to gain what is clearly not worth winning. The result of this expenditure of the earnings and the blood of our commonwealth must inevitably be that our folk will be ground down by the burdens of armaments and war as are the nations of continental Europe.

There is yet another group of considerations bearing on this question that deserves some notice. It is easy to see that the gravest danger to our government arises from the fact that our busy citizens cannot find the time to take a fit share in it. Their employments or their distractions are so engrossing that the commonwealth is of little interest to them; even now our citizens on the average probably do not devote more than the hundredth part of their time to an active care for their government. This inattention to the affairs of the state is a growing evil, — one that may well give all patriots concern, — for to it we may directly trace the degradation of our politics. In the absence of the true citizen the ordinary gain-seeking politician finds his chance. The danger, as is evident, even now with only our internal affairs to occupy our citizens' attention, is that the business of our federal government may pass into the hands of men who seek to make politics a lucrative occupation. If we gain possessions the world about, and so add a great body of foreign affairs to our federal business, we increase the risk of having it all pass into the hands of a governing class. Such, in effect, is the case in Great Britain, where the colonies are governed by a few men, Parliament taking but a very slight interest in what is done with them.

While we can well afford to have professional statesmen, for the work of statecraft demands the whole time of the few men who are fit for it, the professional politicians, men of the sort who seek in government business the chance for gain, are a curse. We have seen much of them in connection with our Indian affairs. Some of these agents have been excellent men, but from the foundations of our government they have as a group been a disgrace to this country. Men in such positions, dealing with folk who are not citizens, cannot be efficiently supervised when the temptations to wrong-doing are great. It is said that we shall organise a corps of officers for the administration of our foreign provinces, — men of character as high as those who do like work for Great Britain, — and that all will thus be well with our subjects who have to depend on these men as representatives of their far-off masters. But these ex-

FOREIGN POSSESSIONS

cellent men will have to be paid not only for their arduous service, but for the years of expatriation in unwholesome countries. The English wage for such duty is high, — far higher than we pay, or are likely ever to pay, such servants of our government. However, and this is the main inducement that enables Great Britain to command her best talent for colonial administration, highly prized official honours are always the reward of success in such work. The coveted Star of India, knighthood, or even a peerage, may by British officers be looked forward to as a crown at the end of a life spent in the faithful discharge of duty. With us the pay for capacity has to be in money, or if that is not given we have to put up with agents of more or less distinguished incapacity with a disposition to seek dishonest gains.

Putting aside the fictitious sense of wealth which the thought of great possessions beyond the sea inspires, looking at the matter in the light of duty and expediency, it clearly appears that we should condemn the policy which leads us on that dangerous way. So far as we need coaling stations for our ships in the far seas, we can easily obtain them under conditions that will not make us rulers of any alien people. If needs be, these harbours may be defended by fortifications, so that in case of war they shall be safe refuges for our ships. Where, as in the Sandwich Islands or Porto Rico, it appears that the countries might be a source of danger to us if they were to fall into the hands of any great military or naval power, it might be well to guarantee their independence, which, so long as we were unassailable as we were five years ago in our continental fortress, would deter any European state from assailing them. As guarantors of their freedom, we would have a helpful influence over such weaker states, that no conquest with arms can possibly give.

CHAPTER XIII

THE CITIZEN AND CITY GOVERNMENT

THE plan of the democratic government rests, as has more than once been said, on the sympathetic understanding of man with man as to those things which should be done in common. Such a government can best be had in a community so small that every one in it has some acquaintance with every other. It is, however, practicable for men to associate themselves in a real democracy when the members of the association are not thus known to one another, provided they all are confident of mutual understandings and purposes, — of the patriotic motives and objects of their unseen fellow-citizens. Thus for a man to be a true citizen of this republic, it is well that he should spend the years in which he acquires his political habits in the country or in a small town where he may become acquainted with many men, and thus have a chance to learn how government arises, and from intercourse gain the confidence in the citizenly integrity of others whom he cannot know.

In the conditions of a great city it is wellnigh impossible for a youth to acquire that unrecognised, almost instinctive confidence in and understanding of his fellow-men that is the foundation of our American political life. He then comes in contact with a number of persons who have the true citizenly quality; but he sees that they are surrounded, in a way overwhelmed, by a throng of folk who, though they may be voters, are in all citizenly quality entirely foreign to our people, with motives that have been acquired in centuries of despotism, and with no chance of ever acquiring the spirit of our country. He is likely to find the control of the place in the hands of its permanently foreign residents or of their essentially unnaturalised descendants. The true American ideals of a "government of the people, by the people, for the people" were replaced by the ancient aristocratic plan of control by a chief, and for plunder, — in effect, a return to iniquities which our forefathers swept away. Painful as these conditions are to every true citizen, he will not be led by them to despair of our methods of government. He will scrutinise these evils, and assail them as it is his business to do in all like crises.

In examining into the conditions of our ill-governed cities, the first point to notice is that their ill condition does not indicate anything like a breakdown of our plan of governing, but in most instances has been brought about by people who have not been educated in the motives and understanding of democracy. In the case of only a few ring-ridden towns the mis-

CITY GOVERNMENT

rule has to be laid to the charge of native-born Americans, who appear never to have acquired the better motives of their country. It is, moreover, evident that while the existence of misgovernment in a city is a disgrace to the commonwealth in which it lies, the iniquity does not often extend to the country about it. The diseased state is evidently promoted by the conditions which exist in these crowded places, where the better men have little chance to affect the actions of the poorer sort.

No one can examine into the conditions of our misgoverned cities without coming to see that a part of the trouble arises from the fact that the political business of the place is done in the name of one or the other of the national parties. The candidates are nominated by Democratic or Republican conventions, and the control of the town is in the hands of the local managers of these parties. This may seem at first sight to be a natural and advantageous arrangement, as it saves the expense and trouble of having separate organisations especially devoted to local questions; it might also be supposed that the managers of these national organisations would be careful so to conduct the affairs of the town that they would win credit for their parties. Much costly experience, however, shows us that whichever party is in power, it uses the offices of the city to help its dependants, and in that way to add to its strength in state or national affairs. Every such association naturally gathers about itself many greedy men who see no other object in politics save personal profit, if not mere plunder. The leaders, who may be above the baser work, feel that they must have the support of these scoundrels: they therefore maintain them, and thus share in their villanies.

It might at first sight be thought that citizens' parties, organised without reference to national politics, would have the same evils arising from the presence of the "workers" that have been encountered in those which are permanent. That this is not the case is shown by much experience. The writer has in mind an instance personally known to me, where, after years of serious trouble with the administration of one or the other of the political parties, an association of citizens determined to establish a nonpartisan party, having for its object the maintenance of an honest and effective administration. Twenty years of experience with this system has shown that it is eminently successful. It may be expected that the worse elements of both of the national organisations will to the utmost oppose the institution of nonpartisan government in our cities; but it clearly is one of the means by which the government of our great cities may be brought out of shame.

It is not to be supposed that the government of our cities can be bettered by at once seeking a non-partisan system of electing their officers. This and other good political work depends on an awakening of their worthy people to a sense of citizenly duty. In part because the people of our great towns are much busier than are the dwellers in less crowded places, in part because they do not know one another as the folk of the country do, they are, in general, much less citizenly. In a way, they all tend to become undemocratic in that they accept without question the iniquities of any government that is imposed upon them. If they had a fair share of patriotic motives, they would revolt against such oppression. So far has this abandonment of the citizenly spirit gone that a large proportion of those native-born persons whose names are on the voting list in our largest towns are in effect foreigners and should be denied the franchise. Some inquiry has led the writer to the opinion that not more than one out of five of the educated and so-called well-to-do men in our great cities have a wholesome interest in their welfare. While they may vote in municipal elections, relatively few of them are disposed to make any kind of sacrifice to do their duty effectively. Therefore the first task of the young citizen is to see how he can help to awaken these inert people to a sense of their duty by their fellows, and by those who are to come after them.

It is well to recognise the fact that the way of the reformer is not easy. He has no longer to fear for life or liberty, but he has to meet the opposition of inattention or the mild contempt with which "practical" people visit the endeavours of those who are fighting the evils about them. He will be asked why he is not about his business — as if there were business in the world better fitted to command a man than that of helping to preserve his government!

It may be assumed that a young man working alone cannot do much to help better the conditions of a city. If he be rich, well placed, and able, he may prove an effective leader, — one who can draw the well disposed to him. But if he has to make his way, he needs to act with others. He will, it is evident, have to do his work outside of the political parties. He may find that there is some citizens' association wherewith he can work. If there is no such organisation, let him begin one by gathering about him those of his friends who are willing to join in the labour. However few its numbers, if the society goes vigorously to work it will assuredly prosper.

As for the methods of such a society, these will have to be fitted somewhat to local needs; but as the first object of the association is to develop the spirit of citizenship, the immediate aim will have to be educative. The way of beginning is by a study of the actual conditions of the town: not only or mainly in those features which are representable by statistics, but rather concerning the way in which the administrative machinery works or fails to work; and especially the condition of the poorer and more helpless people as affected by the city government. The foremost aim should be to seek out and educate for citizenship all the abler men of the so-called

CITY GOVERNMENT

labouring classes, particularly those who are young; for an oldish man of the lower ranks rarely can be helped in this regard. It is always to be remembered that foreigners, at least those of our own race, are apt to have in them the making of good Americans. If the capable men of foreign blood could be really awakened to a sense of their citizenly duty and instructed as to the methods of performing it, there would be better ground for hope as to the future of our cities than we now find. It is well to beware of the common notion that much good can be done in political education by means of instructive lectures given to the people who need help in such matters. The only valuable resources are personal labour with the individual, — so directed as to establish the beginnings of friendly relations, which are the basis of political action, — and debate as to the methods by which betterments may be obtained.

The greatest obstacle to be encountered in an effort to break up the control which the so-called rings have established in our cities arises from the fact that these organisations are very helpful to their members, not only in giving them places and a chance to win money, but through the kindly mutual interest which they develop among their members. It is a mistake to suppose that sympathetic motives are limited to high-minded people; they are often more active and efficient among societies of thieves than they are in those that gather under church roofs. Thus the foreigner who enters Tammany Hall finds himself in a hospitable place, where he is under strong and helpful men who protect him from the ills of hunger and loneliness. He does just what his ancestors have done through the ages: he finds a strong man who has gathered strength about him, and swears allegiance to him, fights his battles, and feeds on what he helped his master to capture. All this is very natural to the primitive man; it is what our ancestors did for ages, while they were the servants of nobles of various degrees. It is the ancient state from which it was the happy fortune of our people to escape, — the state to which we ever tend to return as soon as we relax our efforts to go forward. The only way to maintain this advance in our cities, where foreign immigration is continually introducing these undemocratic folk, is to develop the American motive in the abler men by all the means that make for an education in citizenship. We may trust the public schools for some small part of this work. If those schools brought about any considerable mingling of the native children with those of foreign parentage, we could trust them for much; but in these schools the foreign element is almost always herded together, so that, except for the personal contact with the teachers and a little formal instruction, there is nothing to bring about a naturalising process. While these influences are good, they are entirely insufficient to prevail against the ancient traditions that lead these foreigners to revere and obey " the boss," who is to them what the baron, the prince, or other feudal lord was to their ancestors.

So far as the young citizen aids the young men of foreign stock to become truly naturalised by attaching himself to them and leading them into sympathetic relations with the citizenly folk, he will effectively aid in bettering the government of his city. On this basis of friendly relations it will be possible to bring the abler foreigners to conditions where they may have a chance to acquire our method of looking at the problems of government. To further this education there is nothing like debate concerning the plans and methods of administration, such as our cities present. Any society that essays such debate will of course have some trouble from the Socialists and Nihilists, — people who will bring to it their plans for the reform of government through its destruction. It should be remembered, however, that, while the schemes of these people are undemocratic and often abominable, they all show a spirit of revolt against oppression, that lacks only knowledge to become sound patriotism. Even a bomb-throwing Nihilist, who is willing to sacrifice himself for his convictions, is in a fairer way of becoming a good citizen than those respectable traitors who do not bother themselves even to vote, and contemn the work of the reformer. The only American way of setting these people aside is by debate.

It cannot be too strongly impressed on the young citizen, to whom his city has to look for salvation, that he should not expect to make his career in politics. If he be a man of independent means, he may fitly give his life to the good work. If he has his bread to earn, he should win it outside of politics. It may come about that it is his duty to take office, but he should bear in mind the fact that as soon as he becomes a salaried public servant his influence as a champion of reform will be greatly diminished. When by long service as a plain citizen he has established his position as an independent helper of his people, when his acceptance of a place clearly means to him not profit but loss, then only can he fitly become a public official.

A young man is likely to hear that it will not be possible for him properly to attend to a business by which he is to win his bread and at the same time to do any helpful work in politics. It is true that he cannot serve his people as effectively as he might, were he a man of leisure, but, as the experience of many shows, without any harm to his professional duties can he accomplish much good. The work of any dutifully followed calling teaches a man how to save time and to effect results with a minimum of effort. Moreover, most young men of business have a considerable part of their time at their disposal. That which commonly goes to the idle life of clubs, or the like, is ample for political work such as his city in her need has him do. Moreover, the business man, whatever his vocation, will find in such helpful life among his neighbours, with the large outlooks and friendly relations it establishes, a refreshment from his daily labour.

GOVERNMENT AND THE HAPPINESS OF MAN

The aim of all government is to insure the happiness of the people it controls. The goodness of its methods may fairly be judged by the success with which this end is attained. It is easy to see that the direct effect of government in making people happy cannot be great; it is rather in the things it prevents than in those it brings about that a state contributes to the happiness of society.

The first of all political aims is to give the people a sense of freedom, for no man of spirit can be happy if he feels himself oppressed. If he cannot do the things he is strongly moved to do, and which he knows to be right, he is miserable: however well he may be fed and lodged, he feels that he cannot make his career, that he is in effect a slave. Therefore the first duty of a state is to see that men are as far as possible left free to do as they will. The great art of government is to control people as little as may be.

The next duty of government is to guard people against the dangers of violence. Life at best is troubled with many dangers,—those of poverty, sickness, and of certain death. The aim of government should be to abolish all dangers of violence, whether from acts of criminals, thieves, and murderers, as well as those due to carelessness. War, as the most extended form of violence, it should be one of the first objects of decent governments to avoid. A government that allows wars to occur, except when they are to protect against worse evils, fails of its duty.

Viewed in this way, we find that the state has for its most important functions those which may be termed protective. These functions resemble those of a police or a fire department in a well-organised town. They do not make people happy, but they enable them to seek happiness for themselves, each according to his or her liking and opportunities.

If we follow out the other features of government work, we find that they all come to the same end: they allow people to go their own way in safety and to find their satisfaction according to their desires. In certain countries the state provides in the large cities a part of the expense of great theatres; in our own the various city governments often maintain museums and public parks. But these exceptional acts, good as they are, affect but few of the citizens; they are not of much influence on the total happiness of the people.

There are, unhappily, many miserable persons in every state who, lacking the pleasure which they feel to be their due, think that the wrong is in the government which is over them; that if it were managed better, they would be richer and happier. Such folk make of the state an idol, which they are disposed, after the manner of savages, to beat whenever the world goes ill with them. They need to learn that the government can do no more than to leave a man free to go his way and to give him certain chances of education which may help him on the course which he has to choose and follow for himself. The state may mar his fate; it cannot do much to make it fortunate.

There are, however, certain ways in which citizens, apart from the government work, can help by their associated action to improve the lot of men, and thus to increase the measure of happiness. As we study society we see that a great deal of the best work — that which contributes the most to the happiness of men — is performed in associations that grow up among them. Some of these societies, like the mutual insurance companies or the savings banks, have only a business purpose; others, like the social clubs, propose merely to add to the comfort of their members; yet others, such as the reading and dramatic associations, seek intellectual pleasure and culture as their ends. Although these various guilds and clubs have some disadvantage in that they do not include all the citizens of a neighbourhood, and so give rise to a certain amount of hard feeling, they are as a whole productive of much good, for the reason that, like the churches, they bring people together and teach them to labour for a common cause.

The habit of forming societies or guilds is very ancient; such exist among almost all savages and barbarian states. In this primitive form they are commonly secret, for the reason that uneducated peoples have a great fancy for mystery. This secret quality characterises the greater number of the societies which have come down to us from antiquity. It has been supposed by some people that these associations are a danger to liberty, for the reason that the members are in a way bound to support and protect one another, but there is no evidence that there is any foundation for this view. There have been efforts to found political associations on this secret system. One of them, the so-called " Know Nothings," about forty years ago had a certain brief prominence in its efforts to oppose the Roman Catholic Church; but the people of this country, imbued with the modern spirit of open dealing, soon discarded that party. In any period of intense political excitement these secret political societies are certain to spring up, but experience shows that they are equally certain to pass away under the influences which wisely lead our people to desire publicity in all that relates to the state.

At the point where the state ceases to act for the protection of its members, the individual citizen can in his private capacity continue the good work; he

THE HAPPINESS OF MAN 275

may well take a large part in fostering those associations for various kinds of mutual benefit. There is great room for choice as to what kinds of associations a man may well devote himself; there are certain evident rules which may serve to guide our action in this matter. It is clear that those associations which, like ordinary clubs, have no higher aim than to enable their members to obtain a larger share of comfort and luxury than they would have at home, are of no great use to the people, — they have, indeed, no moral value whatever, and, owing to the fact that they draw men away from their firesides, are often injurious to their members and to the society in which they exist. Those associations which have intellectual culture for their aim are on a far higher level than the merely social clubs; they are in their influence like the schools, — they elevate the life of a community. It is when the societies propose to do some manner of good to people who are not of its fraternity that these institutions attain the highest grade, and this for the simple reason that the best work we do is done for others.

It may be hoped that already the reader will have asked himself the question as to what any man in his quality of a citizen has to do with those matters which are beyond the province of the government. The question is pertinent and the answer important. This is that the citizen is, first of all, a caretaker of the society in which he dwells; he acts with the state in this task, for the reason that the state is the most important contrivance for protecting and helping the people, for giving them a fair chance to live as they have a mind to. This primary duty accomplished, he turns to the other ways of helping men, — to all, indeed, in which they may be aided in their pursuit of true happiness; the state can give no more than an opportunity for this search for the good of life. We thus see that the work of the citizen is but begun when he has done the political part of his duties.

The current of the society in which he lives will generally lead an active-minded citizen to do the non-political part of his work in a good way. If he is to be a leader of his people, it will, however, be necessary for him to look ahead to see among the things that are not done what it is best to undertake. In the greater part of this country the most evident need is of effective societies which shall aim at bettering the intellectual condition of the people, so that they may not, as many do, lose all interest in matters of culture as soon as they leave school, assuming, indeed, that they have gained such interests in their schooling. If this intellectual culture can be increased it is patriotism to bring patriotism and other good qualities with it.

Next after the societies of culture, if they should not be placed first, are the charitable associations.

Their possible second place is due to the fact that charity is often most effective without the aid of societies. Third in order of value we may put a peculiar kind of society, such as is beginning to be formed in this country, having for a purpose the preservation and enhancement of the natural beauty of the country. Few of us recognise how great is the value of this beauty which nature offers us; those who have been educated as all should be to appreciate this charm, find in it a source of enduring joy; it may be indeed a very large element in happiness and in that culture which adds dignity and peace to life.

Although the world is beautiful in its wilderness state, its charm is greatly enhanced by the hand of man, if his work of changing its natural aspect is properly done. Good roads, clean, well-tilled fields, houses of a simple yet attractive character, not offensively staring in colour or decoration, bits of woodland so left as to preserve the native quality of streams and cliffs, may give to the people of a country landscapes the beholding of which will serve to develop a sense of the beautiful without which life, however good in other regards, is sadly incomplete. It should be the aim of the citizen to help to secure these simple means of adding to the happiness of men.

Although the American people are richly endowed with the greater part of the qualities which go to make men happy, they distinctly lack those which relate to the appreciation of beauty. This defect is due in the main to the fact that they have been compelled to look to the practical side of affairs. As pioneers in a new world they have turned to the earth for food and raiment rather than for the perceptions and understandings which should elevate men when they contemplate the beauty and majesty of a landscape. Now that they have won their fruitful land to use and have attained an enviable prosperity, they should seek the elements of happiness which a sympathetic relation to the nature about them can give. The best way to this is through a care for the scenery in which they live; as they come to guard it they will perceive its beauty and have the pleasure which it can lend with the care they bestow.

We cannot expect for a long time to come to possess the art galleries or the great architecture of Europe. It is not in the spirit of a democracy to spend much public money on these attractive things, and private gifts from rich people tend, as they should do, rather to purposes of charity and education than to monumental buildings or to great collections of art objects. But in the beautiful nature of our country we have resources which, if properly used, may become precious means for cultivating the spirit of man. If we properly use these opportunities; if our people come to feel that every marring of natural beauty is a wrong done to them and to those who are to come after them, — we may develop a fitter and more profitable artistic sense than any other nation has acquired. Therefore we may urge as patriotic the endeavour of every citizen to preserve and enhance the charm which belongs to the land about him. In the trees and brooks of this country, to take no account of the larger elements of its scenery, there is a wealth of beauty which, if it could be brought home to the people, would enrich their lives in a way that mere wealth can never do.

THE MANNERS OF THE CITIZEN

It is commonly charged by those who set aristocratic society above democratic that the manners or ways of intercourse of the peoples in republics are bad; that they are lacking in those qualities of respect of one man for another and of the tokens of such respect even where it is felt, which not only give an outward charm to life, but serve to stimulate the sympathies of men. It cannot be denied that there is a certain justice in this criticism. Our people, like the Swiss and to a certain extent the English, usually have a way of meeting their fellow-men which does not truly indicate the state of their feeling towards them. As the aim of men should be to show themselves truthfully to those about them, this rudeness in appearance when they are at heart considerate, this boorish manner when they are really gentle, is wrong; it is a kind of lying for an American, who is really, as the writer knows full well, the gentlest of men to put on the manners of a churlish person.

The general giving up of all attention to good manners by our people, though they had in such leaders as Washington men of most admirable address, was doubtless due to the fact that the ancient modes of intercourse were framed on the customs of an aristocratic society where men were taught to show a false, because purely formal, respect to those who were above them in social station. As the democratic feeling increased, and with it the desire to be honest, men gave up to a great extent the habit of polite and complimentary address. It became the rule of certain sects not to use such words as " sir," " madam," or even " mister," lest they should seem to say more than they meant.

To most people who are in the first stages of democratic culture, and very generally to those who have just escaped from the state where they had to show a certain rather servile civility to superiors, the strongest feeling of their new-found liberty is that " I am as good as you." The later and higher stage of the moral station of the free man, that in which he has the freedom of the Christian gentleman, is that "you are as good as me." There is a vast progress in the passage from the one to the other of these two states of mind: in the first the man still feels the bruises of the chains he has worn; in

MANNERS OF THE CITIZEN

the latter he is emancipated even from the memories of his ancient subjection. Among our people there is still enough of the old revolt against formal respect to those above them to bring about a presentation of themselves to their neighbours which is in its way as untrue as the ancient excess of seeming courtesy. In striving to avoid being false in one way, they have become false in another.

A little consideration of the subject of manners will show that the matter is of sufficient importance to lift it to the level of citizenly duty and accomplishment. When two human beings come to deal with each other in any way, the first thing to be done is for them to find their common mind. If they have citizenly — we may as well say Christian — motives they will approach each other in a friendly, sympathetic humour. It is a common law among the higher animals as well as among men that this good-natured state of mind should, when it exists, be indicated by some forms of action or speech. Even a dog salutes you with certain indications of courtesy if, though you be a stranger, he wishes you well. Often indeed a man's dog shows more of this primitive politeness than his master.

The aim of manners is to afford a kind of bridge over the gulf which separates man from man, so that people may, at their need, pass over it to deal with their neighbours. We each live in ourselves as in a kind of castle. When the other person approaches, if he finds the drawbridge up, the portcullis down, and the warder silent at the gate, he is likely to turn aside; or if he be of a quarrelsome humour he may attack the defences if only to show his displeasure at the cold and unmannerly reception. If he finds welcome at the portal, he enters, or it may be, remains outside, as a friend. In a democracy where so much depends upon a good understanding between men, when every important act requires that they come quickly each to see what the other means, it is peculiarly important that ways of passage be kept open between those who have to work together. Thus though manners may have been mere ceremony in an aristocracy, they are substantial things in a society such as our own.

While formal salutations should not be excessive and thereby untrue, they should take a distinct shape and be clearly understood by those who use them. Thus the phrase "good-morning," the simplest of the old greetings that survive, did not really mean, as some suppose, that the day was in itself good, but a natural wish that it might prove so to the person who was saluted. It served to open or close the intercourse in a human way. The habit of lifting the hat to women or to other respected people is a familiar token of esteem, once full of meaning, for it indicated the removal of the helmet or other armour from the head; the grasping of hands, which deprived both of the chance to use the sword, is another token of an

MANNERS OF THE CITIZEN 283

ancient state of man. All these forms, when sensibly used, not only signify our good humour to others, but they serve as signals to our own minds, rousing them to a friendly state. Every one has had a chance to see how easy it is to bring about a certain way of thinking or feeling by putting on the manner which belongs to that state of mind. Prince Henry in his speech to his troops recognises that soldiers may help to make themselves brave by behaving as though they were so. In his exhortations before the battle Shakespere makes him say, —

> ". . . Stiffen the sinews, summon up the blood,
> Now lend the eye a terrible aspect."

Manners at their best indicate the benevolence of the mind and help to insure that admirable quality in our relations with our fellow-men. They are the best of all passports for the man who would go forth to his neighbours, the truest test of that large quality which is indicated by the word "gentleman." Therefore every citizen should have good manners even as he should be able to talk, read, and write as a part of his fitting for the ordinary duties of life. The fact that the citizen of a true democracy has no station but that which he has made for himself, and is continually renewing, renders it more necessary that he should have the nature and manners of a gentleman than it does for the aristocrat to have those qualities; for the nobleman has his station determined by his birth, while we of the new order have it as the gift of each person with whom we come in contact.

If a person seeing the noble and useful quality of good manners desires to acquire the art and habit of them, let him begin by taking care that he approaches his neighbour in a truly friendly spirit, — not greedily or with a desire to command him, but in a disinterested, sympathetic spirit with a perfect willingness to hear him first and to consider what he has to say. The mere forms of civility have little importance except so far as they are accepted tokens which have the convenience that everybody understands them alike, so that they have become signs of a state of mind, a kind of shorthand of human intercourse, but as signals of our state of mind they serve as words do to help us to understand our neighbour. Therefore we should so seek to shape our manners that they may enable us graciously to approach those who share the world with us. A man should be ashamed to find he cannot come near to others of his kind or even to a dog in a way to disarm suspicion.

A failure to have a good-mannered state of mind, and to express that state in a way that the neighbour understands it and feels it to be sincere, is, in the experience of the writer, who has had a long experience with young men at a large school, the commonest source of ill success in life. Men of distinguished quality remain shut up as in a prison whose walls they cannot see and hardly feel except when they

MANNERS OF THE CITIZEN

wonder what ails them in their relations with their fellows. Yet that institution has the well-deserved reputation of being among other things a good school of manners; we may thereby judge how great is the need of reform in this most important of all characteristics of our citizens.

The consideration of the other being, on which foundation rests good manners, cannot be forced into existence at the moment of social contact; it must come as the result of habit that has shaped the man. A man who would effectively mend his mode of contact with persons has most commonly to mend his ways of considering them; he must be habitually in a mannerly humour.

The development of the sympathetic spirit, which affords the basis of good manners, is, or should be, the duty, the very first duty, of teachers of religion, but there are certain simple forms of the training which are closely related to citizenly conduct which may be noted here. A man who lets no occasion go by in which he can mend or avoid marring the conditions which make for the well-being of his neighbours will be in constant training in the great school of manners. This beneficial work may be of a very simple nature; he may merely take the stones from the road which trouble those that pass that way, or avoid throwing waste paper on the street, or in public grounds where it fouls the place and offends those who value its fitness and beauty, or if the chance offers, the deed, though of the same quality, may be larger. The point is that he should constantly and instinctively have in mind the helping of the unseen man. When that spirit is developed, he may be sure that when he appears he is ready for dealings with him.

From the point of view of citizenship the question of manners may be thus briefly stated. It is all-important in the interests of the commonwealth that people should be able to come in easy, friendly contact one with another. This end cannot be attained except by the way of good manners. Such manners are in the main part the expression of a kindly state of mind which will not grow up of itself, but needs devoted culture; all the means of securing this end, in which the goodness of the commonwealth so far depends, deserves the very close attention of every true citizen.

CHAPTER XIV

THE CITIZEN AND HIS FELLOW-MAN

CLEARLY related to the manner in which the citizen meets his fellows of the commonwealth is the larger question concerning the idea he may have as to what an individual man really is and how he is related to the world about him, especially to his fellow-man. At first sight this question seems too large for understanding. It is really very large, — so great, indeed, that most persons do not even see that it exists, yet it is of much importance to every one who would have a right idea of himself and his relations with those who share life with him. To understand something of what a man is we need to look at the processes by which his kind has come to be. This, for our purpose, may be briefly told.

The most important lesson of modern science is that mankind came into this world not by immediate shaping from the dust, but out of the experiences of ancient life; that if we could trace his ancestry backwards through the ages we should find his qualities of mind and body had been developed in the slow but steadfast ascent of life, through perhaps a hundred thousand distinct species of living beings and immeasurably numerous individuals, from the beginning of animal life to the present day. Thus, what is before us in the individual man is not what appears to our eyes, but a record of processes which began probably more than a hundred million years ago, which through an endless process of life and death, of preservation of what was good and destruction of what was bad, has brought the creature to the state of to-day. It is well for us to hold this majestic truth as well as we may in mind, for it will help us to clear away the cheap commonplace idea of ourselves and our fellows, which more than anything else harms our life.

The next point to be noted is that in order to make it possible for living creatures to advance by a process of improvement based on experience in living, it was necessary to have the life of each individual brief; otherwise the earth would soon have been cumbered with lowly forms, and the advance of life towards its higher station, and eventually to man, would have been impossible. So the method of getting rid of the individuals by death as soon as they have had a chance to do their fit part was instituted. It may be asked why the first-made creatures were not kept alive for the ages, and gradually so improved by experience that they could themselves attain the advancement that comes to their successors. We see perhaps a sufficient answer to this question in the way in which we have to deal with our own inventions. We cannot so contrive it that a clock or a steam-engine shall do its appointed work, and at the same time be continuously built over to make it better. The only practical way is to have each do its work, and then be replaced by another which has been improved by experience.

Whatever may have been the need that led to the institution of death, and there may have been many inventions of it, it was clearly required, as we see by the fact that while the first-made lower kinds of life have no fixed duration, but may live on until by some accident they are destroyed, a definite length of life is established in all the species in all the higher classes of animals, so that apart from mischances the individual must die after it has lived for what seems to us a relatively brief time. Thus while the life of a man may endure at the most for about a hundred years, the life of the world, of which it forms a part, has doubtless been in existence for a hundred million years or more; so at most we have for our individual selves the millionth part of the time in which the life of this earth has existed. For our immediate purpose the lesson of this is that the individual man is the noble, though momentary, embodiment of the successes which have been won through the experience of many million ancestors, through which it has found its profitable course from the lowest stage of existence. To those who comprehend this truth the fellow-being appears clothed in a dignity such as was never discovered before science made this clear.

We need also to consider how the process which, through the succession of generations in the life below men, and in the lower men, has given to each individual a share of the qualities, bodily and mental, of all the creatures through which the life was derived. A familiar and often noted instance of this fact, that a man is but a host of inheritances presided over by his higher self, is seen in the survival in the human body of many parts once necessary to the animals through which man came, but now not only useless, but, as in the case of the appendix to the intestines, which may become the seat of disease. These unserviceable parts are all in the way of disappearing; the death they bring about probably helps them out by removing those who have them still in a considerable development. But this survival of unnecessary and now injurious parts and organs, though it indicates something of what inheritance may do to harm, gives no idea of what it has done to help. We need the exercise of the imagination in the light of our knowledge of anatomy and physiology to aid us to this conception. Perhaps the best way to do this is as follows: —

Taking the smallest possible part of the human body we find under the microscope that it is not a mere mass of matter, but is even more completely organised than the whole body appears to be to

HIS FELLOW-MAN 291

the naked eye. It is a wonderful complication of structures of cells, fibres, fluids of very complicated chemical nature, each part guarded by impulses which determine its action much as the will guides the movements of the whole body. Whatever be the nature of this control that sends these infinitesimally small parts on their appointed ways of life, it is perfectly evident that the perfection of this work is due to the experience of the lower life through which man came. In a word, this man whom habit leads us to look upon as a commonplace object has gathered in him the profitable lessons that the innumerable host of ancestors learned in their brief lives and handed on to their descendants through the ages.

What we behold in the body of man and its functions that make up his life is repeated in his mind. His senses, by which he learns what he may concerning the world about him, — eyes, ears, the instruments of touch and taste, — are all animal parts, shaped geological ages ago and in creatures below his present station. So, too, the simple desires and emotions that are related to these instruments, — his rages, fears, hungers, and simple pleasures, — are likewise ancient, for they appear, as we see, in many of the higher animals. In part only is man's intelligence peculiarly his own, for in many of the beasts we find traces of the affections, the sympathies, and even the reason such as he possesses. Thus, while there is a part of his spiritual and rational nature which is essentially unlike anything in the brute, the great body of man's intellectual life was shaped before the earth knew him as man. We thus see that in this supreme individual we have no simple thing, as we are inclined to take him, but a vast complex in which a host of ancient prehuman forms have combined their experience in a tangle that must ever defy the imagination to picture.

Here we should note the fact that in the advance of life from the lower to the higher stages of being the upgoing is not steadfast and certain, but with many halts and stumblings, and often with returns to the lower stage in the ascent. Thus it comes about that only the best of any generation or of any species, a few elected by the fates, attain to the highest or most perfect grade, while others are denied the chance of full development. These *reversions,* as they are called by naturalists, better termed partial successes in advancement, are common in all living species, but most marked in man. Sometimes they lead to only slight bodily defects, as that of harelip, with the cleft palate that goes with it, or the presence of an additional finger or toe; or it may be of very grave character, as when the growth of the brain goes no further than in the ape, with the result that the human side of the mind does not fully develop; and consequently the share of the lower passions and greeds is so excessive that the weak intelligence and sympathies cannot control the creature to a true humanity. We then have the possible criminal, the so-called degenerate, who may be a little better than a beast, masked in the semblance of a man. Experience shows it is usually possible for his more fortunate brethren to help such a defective to win his rightful inheritance by appropriate treatment, much as the surgeon helps those who have too many fingers or harelips. It is, indeed, in this reparation of such defects of body and mind that much of the best work of civilisation may be done.

While our knowledge that the vice and crime of the world is due mainly to the excessive amount of the ancestral brute that is in the criminal folk may fairly awaken our pity for them, it does not justify us in deeming them irresponsible. These ancient impulses to brutality are, though in varying degrees, present in every human being. We may, if we please, term them as they are generally termed, the original sin of man. The naturalist is in perfect agreement with the moralist in believing that every person has to contend against his innate brutalities, for it is by such efforts that man has come to the best of his human quality. He who fails to make the fight must be adjudged a sinner, though in some instances the evil inheritances are so strong that he is hardly to be blamed for not conquering them; in this event he may rightly be considered as irresponsible or insane.

Perhaps the most important truth for us to keep

in mind in our dealings with our fellow-men is the singular nature of their individuality. Each of them is set apart in this world. By the process of development each has inherited an inconceivably great and wonderful store of capacities and qualities of mind and body, — a store which for the moment of its existence represents all the beings through which its life came. Over this marvellous association rules the conscious individual we call the self, receiving through its senses from the outer world what it can, and sending what tokens of itself it may to its neighbours. Yet, for all it can do, it remains strangely apart and lonely in this great universe. In the lower life we see many evidences that the creatures appreciate the loneliness of their individuality for all that are nearly akin to man, — the mammals and birds especially, — and, in less measure, the lower reptiles, amphibians, and fishes seek the society of their kind. Many of the nobler brutes will, if deprived of contact with their kindred, often adopt companions of other species; but this need of friendship, this struggle against the supreme evil of isolation, is most evident in man, for he alone by his consciousness of himself is in a position in adequate measure to feel how lonely he is.

The only way in which this solitary state of the individual can be lessened is by that wonderful process termed sympathy, by which the creature learns that his kinsman feels as he does. In its simplest state we note this sympathy in the flocks and herds of animals where each has comfort in union with his neighbours. We see it also in the mother with her young, which are felt to be a part of herself. We may observe the same motive in children playing with their dolls, which they by their fancy endow with their own motives, or in our treatment of our dogs, on whom we bestow our own qualities. Yet, further, we find it in all our instructive interpretation of nature in which we personify or conceive as human the earth and sky, even the realm of nature itself.

Although the ways in which the loneliness of the individual is lessened are exceedingly varied, the only way in which he can be brought to the station of happiness is by society, — that system of customs or institutions each and all the result of efforts to attain a sympathetic understanding of man with man, so that the otherwise solitary lives may be passed in mutual understandings. The simplest, and in all regards the most important, of the many institutions of society, for it is the foundation of them all, is the family. In it the sense of companionship is the surest, and so the relief of the solitariness is the most complete. So far as the primitive yearning for association goes, that of simple not necessary intellectual companionship, it suffices. But in the great hunger for sympathy there comes a demand for larger associations that are related to the intellectual desires, to the accomplishment of purposes relating to the fate of the fellow-men. Out of this more strictly human group of impulses develop our societies to their fulness in a commonwealth. But while the purposeful rational quality of men gives shape to these institutions, the sympathetic element is, or needs to be, interwoven with the rational to make them in the highest measure helpful to those who dwell under their protection.

The most essential difference between an aristocratic or despotic society and a democracy is to be found in the extent to which they respectively lead to sympathetic relations between the people who compose them. In a pure despotism there can be little of this, for his subjects know only the tyrant's will and their own fears. In an aristocracy the few high-placed folk have this free interchange of motives, but people who form the mass of the society are limited to their family affairs. In a democracy of an ideal kind, such as is never perfectly attained, but is the goal of the true patriot, the sympathies of all citizens go forth to every part of the work of their society and their state. In this way they become most completely united to one another in affections and understandings, and have the largest share of happiness that may come from such union. The association in which they belong is shaped by the impression that every noble life makes on it, and the enduring structure remains the fittest monument of those who have lived and died within it.

HIS FELLOW-MAN

It is by such considerations as to the nature and place of the individual man that we may be prepared to do our part by ourselves and our fellows. From them we learn that our societies are more than they at first sight seem. That all of them — the family circle, the neighbourhood, the town, or the state which includes them — are in effect contrivances whereby this solitary being, man, may have his life united with others of his kind, and be thereby given happiness as well as a chance to grow to his full intellectual and moral stature, and be able to leave more of himself with his kind when he passes away. We see that every action that lessens the value of these elements of our social system is a wrong to mankind.

Not only does a right understanding of the conditions of the individual man help us the better to plan for him, it serves as well to guide us in dealing with various evils which are due to the crude state in which the sympathies have been inherited by man from his brutal ancestors. It is thus easily seen that in all human societies there is a tendency for men to act by a kind of contagion of example much as does a herd of beasts. This is seen in panics, where men commonly rational will suddenly lose their human quality to be possessed by senseless fear, or in mobs where a body of men acting as a pack of wolves will be guilty of cruelties which, if alone, no one of them could do. In fact, in all actions where a number of persons are associated, those who see clearly may discern this ancient lowly form of the sympathies against which he needs to guard himself and others. Our aim should be to help in every way we can to bring about a union of this animal instinct for doing as the fellow-being does with the rational qualities of man. The development of a true commonwealth can only be attained through such a union of the inherited sympathies, and the understanding which gives man his exalted place in the world.

The most important result of our modern learning as to the nature of the individual is, or should be, to give to every one a noble conception of himself and of his relations to his fellow-men. It should at the same time afford him a sound basis of judgment as to the value of our institutions. He will see that all forms of associations are finally to be judged by the measure in which they help the sympathetic relations of men and thereby bring them the happiness such relations may afford, — the only true and enduring happiness they can know. He should see that by this test we may determine the success of every commonwealth, or of its several parts; that the homes, the local and general governments, the churches, the shops, are one and all to be weighed in the balance against the happiness which is the destiny of mankind.

Whoever takes this view of human relations with him into his daily contact with men will be likely to avoid the common mistake of looking upon him-

HIS FELLOW-MAN

self and his fellows as matters of small account. So far as he recognises the true nature of the individual, he will find himself moved to deal with him sympathetically and helpfully. He will see that real citizenship consists in the application of the motives of Christianity to human relations. That religion far more than any other belief has for its foundation the idea of the brotherhood of men, and of the need of their living in affectionate relations with one another. Here at least science and enlightened faith are at one. All that learning, religious or scientific, gives us leads to the same conclusion, which is that the aim of life is to bring men to love one another.

It is easy to see that this understanding of a Christian commonwealth is quite other than that of the ancient state, — that strong brutal power which was conceived, not as exemplifying and embodying the right-doing of its true citizens, but as a might to be imposed on its subjects or used to destroy its rivals. In place of that old hideous view of governments, we are now to regard them as embodiments of the better motives of the men, dead and living, who have given them their character.

It is not sufficient that the citizen merely understands the large basis of his relations with his fellows, for he cannot, under the conditions of his trust, be a mere looker-on in his commonwealth. His part is to force his understandings on his associates, for in that way commonwealths are built and maintained. If he needs to hearten himself for the struggle, let him turn to any of the true heroes of his race, to find that their heroism consisted in a perfect willingness to sacrifice themselves for their convictions.

CHAPTER XV

THE VALUE OF GREAT MEN TO THE CITIZEN

THE citizen who would develop high ideals of his duty and action should make himself familiar with the lives of certain of the great men and women who have shaped his state, his race, or mankind. The choice of these heroes should be made according to one's interest. If this be general, there is no better first book than " Plutarch's Lives " of the famous men of antiquity, which book has been a very fountain of honour for near a hundred generations. If the reader be interested in military men, the biographies of the great captains, such as the admirable series by Col. T. A. Dodge, will serve him well, though, like all other military histories, they tend to give one an exaggerated impression of the place and dignity of war. If the interest is in statesmen, or in the lives of scholarly men, our English literature, which is very rich in biographies, will afford in each field an abundant choice.

Where a person has access to a large library, it is well for him to glance at the lives of many men, so that he may have some idea of their deeds and characters; he can then select a few to be his masters, and of these seek to know all that is known. To do this, he should read, if possible, several different accounts of each life, so that he may have a chance to compare opinions of the men and form his own views.

Properly studied biographies give one by far the best knowledge of history that any but a professional student of the matter is likely to obtain. Thus, any one who knows the lives of Washington, Jefferson, Madison, Jackson, Lincoln, and the other presidents who have been of more than mere political importance, will have unfolded to him all the large affairs of our national life. It is in the quality of a great man to enter into the life of his day in such a manner that his story is, in a way, that of his time. When Dante, in his marvellous poem, tells of his passage through Hell, he describes himself as conducted by the spirit of the poet Virgil; his literary skill taught him that no such strange journey could be imagined as taken without a guide. So, too, when we seek to enter into the realm of the past, we need a guide such as we may select from the great men of each age.

In the course of an ordinary life it is possible, as the writer personally knows, even for one who is much occupied, to gain from books a tolerably good knowledge of some fifty or more great men. The most fortunate of us rarely have a chance to be-

VALUE OF GREAT MEN

hold from near by any man of real greatness. It is true that there is something about a man in the flesh that there is not in the man in the book, but the difference is not really as great as it seems at first sight to be. Our chance to know the truth about the heroic person after he has passed into history is commonly much better than it was while he is living.

From among those men, some hundred in number, who are the well and widely remembered benefactors of our kind, it is best to select a certain few whose lives seem to fit our needs and to afford a pattern of what we would make our own. We should make these men the companions and examples of our doing in such a manner that they become in a way our friends. We cannot expect to copy them, for each life is peculiar; its problems are individual and of its own time; but our heroes serve us as counsellors and guides along many ways which otherwise we have to pass in loneliness. Of all the vast store of good help which human records afford, none other are more precious than the accounts of noble lives.

Where the greatness of men is embodied in their writings, as is the case of the larger number of those who give us much help, the reader will do well to form the habit of committing those parts of their works which seem to him most uplifting, or otherwise helpful, to memory, or, as a more expressive phrase has it, *learning them by heart*. This custom of storing the mind with selections of great poetry or prose, very common in the last generation, has been unhappily much disused in the present day. The gentleman of half a century ago was, if he aspired to culture, expected to memorise many thousand lines of poetry, English and Latin, as well as some of the great orations in those tongues. These treasures he was expected to keep, not in the lumber-rooms of his mind, but so near to his ordinary thought that he would be apt to quote them or shape his thought on them. It is to the effort to give youths too much variety of instruction that we owe the loss of the habit of using the classics of our own and other languages in lifting and lighting our ordinary life.

Those who will provide themselves with clear memories of the noble men to whom we owe the world of affairs as we find it, and will fix their words or deeds in memory, will soon discover that in the many occasions where they need help their hero is there to supply it, — with word of counsel or example. The one way in which a man may most effectively enlarge and ennoble his citizenly quality is by taking to himself the strength which the illustrious dead can give him. Dead though they be, they are often safer guides than the ablest of the living; for, until the work of men is done, we cannot truly gauge its value. If we could weigh the

THE AMERICAN SPIRIT

actions of those who make or save our states, we should most likely find that their success in life and their fame has been due mainly to the fact that into their lives has entered the strength of the great who had gone before them. In other words, success as a citizen depends in large measure on the capacity to gain power from the example of others.

Along with the consideration of our heroes — those blessed individuals who, by their faithful deeds, have helped all men to faith — should go a certain amount of attention to those other men who, by their lack of citizenly motive, have for all their prowess of nature or station been harmful to the state. Fortunately, in our own country we have not many such to set against the masterful helpers we have named as the host of lesser who deserve a place in our list of heroic men. Many have been in some measure harmful to the commonwealth because they lack the ability to see the path of duty, or because they allowed their unreasoning greeds to rule them where reason was called for. In a word, that our shining heroes should appear in all their value, we need for contrast to set against them the men of darkness, — those who allowed their brutal motives to guide them and to harm the commonwealth.

THE AMERICAN SPIRIT

In every people which has made for itself an important place in the world there exists, or has existed, a certain combination of motives in the mass of its people which has served to determine its general character. Thus, while it is not easy to define the difference of motive between the Athenians and Spartans or the Greeks and the Romans, every student of classic times recognises that they are essentially different, as are the English and the French or the Hollander and the German in our own day. These peculiarities of human quality which characterise people are the more distinct in proportion to the importance of the folk in the great association of mankind. It would, indeed, not be difficult to show that to these peculiarities of spirit has in the main been due the share of action which states, ancient and modern, have had for good or evil in the world's affairs. We see this clearly when we note that the intense and high religious motive of the Jews has given to that wonderful folk, which never attained any considerable station in war, commerce, or the arts, a strange dominance over all Western civilisation. It has, moreover, endowed their scattered remnants with a power which abides, after two thousand years of oppression, such as would have utterly crushed a spiritually weaker people.

When we thus recognise the importance of the qualities of peoples, we naturally desire to find what is that of our own, and how far is it likely to affect its future. There are certain reasons why it

THE AMERICAN SPIRIT

is difficult to answer this question as regards the United States: In the first place, history appears to show that it commonly requires five hundred years or more of life under like conditions of climate, food, and custom for a folk to develop its qualities. Some such period elapsed before any of the other great nations of ancient or modern times attained to its characteristics, to those qualities which most distinctly separated it from its neighbours. It has been but two hundred and fifty years since the English colonies in America were founded and began to adapt themselves to life in the new land. It is, indeed, not more than two centuries that this life has begun to develop a distinctive American quality. Therefore, though events including those of the spirit have marched rapidly in the New World, it may be doubted whether there has been time for our national spirit to take its final shape.

We have also to consider the fact that most, if not all, the other peoples that have attained to greatness by their quality have been essentially of the same race or stock; that is, they have been composed of folk that came from one part of the world and were originally much alike. This fact, we may reasonably suppose, made it easier for their descendants to come to the common way of thinking, which forms a rational spirit out of that of a host of individuals which dwell together; for, after all, such spirit is no more than what is common to the separate persons. It is easy to see that in this country we have no such uniformity in the people as existed among the Greeks, Jews, or other folk that have attained a distinct national spirit. On the contrary, while the first colonies founded in this country were of tolerably pure English blood, or that of the closely related Hollanders, we have since taken in a strange mixture of folk, — French, Italians, Spanish, and Africans, — so that quite half our people are of other than English origin. The question arises how far this mixture of diverse kinds of men may prevent or delay growth of a distinct American quality.

The best answer to such doubts as to the development of a definite American quality is to be had by a little observation as to what we now find to be features in our national spirit which differ from those of other countries. It is easy to see that differences, and those of importance, exist; some of them are, indeed, recognised by all careful observers who have studied our people. First among these characteristics of our American folk as regards its distinction and importance, though it has not been recognised by foreigners, is the unexampled confidence which Americans have in their fellow-citizens of the same race and speech, — as between the white men of Maine and Florida, and those of Massachusetts and California, there exists an instinctive sense of fellowship which is practically unhampered, by the fact that they know no more of each other than

THE AMERICAN SPIRIT

that they are all Americans together. In effect, the American of European stock has acquired the habit of looking upon all his fellow-citizens as essentially like himself; in all the ordinary actions of life he expects them to behave as he would under similar conditions. He has, in a word, generally attained to a state of mind concerning his neighbours which is Christian and democratic.

How different is the American belief in the unseen neighbour, as like himself from the state of mind in the Old World, can only be judged by those who know the peoples on both sides of the Atlantic. In the Old World we find, even in England, where the folk are most akin to our own, a more evident lack of sympathetic understanding or even distinct distrust between neighbouring countries than can be found among the most widely separated parts of this country. On the continent of Europe this disbelief in the fellow-man is much more evident than in Great Britain. Nowhere do men trust their unseen fellow-citizens as we of America do; and when we come to the region bordering the Mediterranean Sea, the folk of one valley appear generally to believe that their neighbours on the other side of the divide, with whom they have no acquaintance, are really dangerous people.

It is easy to see that the American's confidence in others of his kind is in large measure due to the fact that they never have harmed him, while the lack of it in the Old World is to be accounted for by the fact that there in past ages, indeed, until modern times, the usual condition was that of war between neighbouring communities. Separated from this ancient evil of contention, the people of English-America have been left free to develop a sound human confidence in their fellow-citizens such as never before existed among widely separated men. It is also evident that this state of mind is most important to the future of our nation, as it assures a degree of unity which no laws or customs could possibly bring about. When we look for the basis of our national success, and for the foundation of the greatness to come, we find it most assuredly in this mutual understanding and belief in our kinship of character. A striking instance of its value is presented by the history of our Civil War; as this is the best of all the great lessons of that memorable conflict, we should see it clearly.

In the years before the war between the states there grew up a body of doubts and hatred which promised to separate the people of the North and South in the manner in which the nations of the Old World are parted. For a time, indeed, this difference was distinct: the people of one section distrusting the motives of the other, each believing the other to be different in kind from their own. When war came the folk of these opposed sections of the country were thrown into a rude yet effective contact. Each learned that the other was brave and devoted to duty. In the innumerable chances of friendly meetings which this war gave, the men of both sides had the good chance to find that they were, after all, not far apart in their essential qualities. It was perhaps the only great conflict which helped the combatants to a mutual understanding.

At the end of the Civil War the old animosities between the people of the two sections had to a great extent been cleared away, so that, but for the plans of certain political leaders and the trouble that lurked in the questions as to the future relations of the whites with the freed negroes, a true reunion between the sections would have at once come about. Unhappily, the action of Congress and of a host of scoundrels who were given authority over the southern people by that action led to a period of tyranny and plunder in the seceding states which will ever be a shame to our nation. The only redeeming feature of this dark time in our history is to be found in the confidence of the southern folk — a trust that proved to be well placed — that their northern brethren, their conquerors, would make an end of these evils as soon as they had a chance to do so. They were, in fact, thus ended as soon as the people of the north were able to take their measure. Thus, although the iniquities of the so-called work of reconstruction had been in many ways greater than those of the war, the path was soon opened for a true reconstruction of the Union on the sound American basis of mutual understanding and respect.

As it has been before said, the Civil War, as a matter of fighting, has, to those who would understand our American people, only a secondary importance; but the debates concerning the question of slavery and state rights which preceded the conflict tell much of the spirit of our people, and even more is revealed by the wonderful swiftness with which a mutual understanding was attained by the combatants after the work of arms was done. Never before in the history of man has such a conflict been waged to end in a firmly established peace. The steps that led to this reconciliation shows the spiritual bond which unites our people in mutual confidence, — a bond that the fiercest struggle of modern times only served to reaffirm. This contest also shows another quality which is distinctively American; that is, a willingness to fight for ideals of society and government such as have rarely, if ever, entered into the conflicts of the Old World. Elsewhere and in all times men have fought for chieftains, for dynasties, for national power, for religious beliefs, or, oftenest, because of mere hatreds; but this characteristically American conflict was mainly for ideals as to social and political organisations, — whether the supreme authority of our Union should lie in the national or the state government, and

THE AMERICAN SPIRIT 313

whether the people of the alien African race should be held as slaves or as ordinary work people, are held by their employers. The fact that the Civil War was fought to determine such large citizenly questions in a way serves to mitigate the disgrace that it should have been fought at all, and in some measure to reconcile us to the vast and irreparable losses which it entailed.

The way in which our people dealt with the questions which led to and followed the Civil War shows that there exists in them another quality besides the confidence in their fellow-men and the high ideals of society and government which we have just noted. This is a certain confidence in and willingness to accept the result of a popular judgment on any matter which has been well debated. If we look over the history of other peoples, we find that about the worst, or at least the commonest, of their misfortunes arose from the unwillingness of large minorities to accept the judgments of courts, elections, or battles as decisive and as fully making an end of debate in the matter in hand. These minorities commonly hold to their purposes, and after the manner of the followers of the exiled Stuart of England or the Bonapartists in France, prove a long-continued danger to their states. But with us, as the results of the Civil War showed, the people have accepted the most important point of democratic government, which is that the decisions of a debate are to be accepted, that idle fighting is not to be tolerated.

This prompt acceptance of judgments, such as those of their supreme court, of their important elections, and of the great contest of the Civil War, clearly indicate that the masses of men in this country have a measure of discernment which elsewhere is found only in people trained in diplomacy. It marks a distinct advance in the state of the public mind beyond what has been attained in earlier ages or concerning other peoples of our time. Its effects are not only to be found in matters of large politics, but in lesser affairs as well. They are to be noted in the methods of business, where men quickly abandon old methods or machines as soon as they have been found less useful than the new, or change from one religious faith to another, as the claims of the several churches impress them. In a word, American men have evidently come to a state of mind where their actions are singularly little controlled by traditions and prejudices, where they are, as no other body of folk ever has been, free to act swiftly and together.

Along with his independence of judgment, and closely related therewith, the American in general exhibits a gentleness towards men he regards as of his own kind, and whom he instinctively considers as closely akin to himself. This was well shown during the Civil War by thousands of instances in

THE AMERICAN SPIRIT

which the soldiers of all grades exhibited a human interest in their official enemies. The result was that with few exceptions the campaigns of that war were marked by an absence of the unnecessary cruelty which has so often disgraced the work of soldiers. We find the same absence of brutality in the treatment of the surrendered Confederate armies and their statesmen as well. From the point of view of the law, all these people were guilty of treason, and were liable to pay the penalty for it with their lives; yet by common consent, and practically without debate, all idea of legal process against them was abandoned. Not a single man was brought to trial for treason; and the imprisonment of Jefferson Davis, the sometime president of the Confederate states, met with such general condemnation in the north that he was quickly set free, — to spend the remainder of his life in publicly abusing his conquerors. The most of the other leaders of the Confederacy promptly found honoured places in Congress, in the federal courts, or in the executive government. When they were not too aged for service, they were given fit stations in the armies of the Spanish War, and this by the party which had held power during the war of secession. In a word, the treatment of the southern people, except for the miserable political blunders and their train of woes of the reconstruction period, for which the body of the northern people were not blameworthy, show that our folk have in them an essential gentleness of spirit in all that regards their own people, the like of which has not existed elsewhere among men.

Although the people of this country are in a way peculiarly merciful to those they feel to be their neighbours, and carry the idea of neighbourliness very far, this motive has a singular limitation, for it does not extend beyond certain arbitrary and curious bounds. While he is easily and spontaneously moved to sympathy with all those whom he regards as of his own people, as of himself in other form, the American in general is, by his instinctive dislike of all other races, curiously incapable of anything like generous treatment of them. Unlike the Spanish and French, and even the English, he never in any general way entered on friendly relations with the aborigines of this country. In fact, our treatment of the Indians, if taken alone, would stamp our folk as one of the most brutal of modern times. Something of the same incapacity to feel for or with people of alien race is seen in the attacks that have been made on the Chinese of the far West, — outbreaks of a fiendish nature not paralleled elsewhere among civilised people for a hundred years or more. Again, in the lynchings of murderers which are so disgracefully common in the West and the South, we find characteristic men of our race for the moment acting as demons, denying, as it were, all kinship with the gentle quality which is so well shown

THE AMERICAN SPIRIT

in the history of our Civil War. The fact seems to be that the American's good-nature is due to an instinctive belief in the likeness of the men about him to himself. When this idea of kinship is lacking for the reason that the fellow-man has a peculiar colour, or has done something that a decent man cannot conceive a human being guilty of doing, all sense of common humanity may be at once lost, and the American becomes the most brutal of civilised men.

It has often been remarked that the British folk, for all their wonderful successes in governing other races, have achieved their results, not by understanding or sympathising with the aliens they rule, but solely by their honesty and strength. Unlike the French and Spaniards, who readily come to friendly relations with savages, the British always remain essentially their conquerors. This feature of the Anglo-Saxon character, if we may judge by the behaviour of the American with the folk of other races with whom they have come in contact, has in some way been intensified in our people.

We find the best evidence as to the narrowness of American sympathies not in the way in which our people have dealt with the Indians, but in our conduct towards the negroes. In the case of the Indians, there has always been difficulty in associating with them because of the difference in language; few, if any, pure-blooded aborigines have ever spoken English well, and probably not a thousand white men of our race have ever been able to speak an Indian tongue with ease. The difference of customs and traditions was in itself a serious barrier to friendly relations. Moreover, our people were compelled to deprive the Indians of their birthright in the country, and thus to become their enemies. Thus much of the unhappy history of the relations between our folk and the aborigines was inevitable. It is otherwise in our relations with the negroes; all these people, though they belonged to many different races and tribes, have proved to be remarkably docile; they quickly and effectively acquired our language and in a singularly complete way became separated from their primitive customs and traditions; so that, except for some inborn natural qualities of mind, they have become very perfect imitations of ourselves.

So far as the treatment of the Africans while they were slaves is concerned, there is not very much to be said in the way of condemnation. Slavery is inevitably evil, but it is evident that a people of an alien race has never fared better in such a station. Their masters were generally humane and careful of their welfare. In general, those of our folk who had the responsibility of the master learned to have a real affection for the negro and to feel for him as a man. It has been and still is quite otherwise with those of our people who have never been thrown into close personal relations with the blacks. To them this African race is absolutely alien; they have no instinctive sympathy with its people; they are, indeed, commonly repelled by the differences of colour and face. In general, the white people of this country desire that the black man shall have all the legal rights of the citizen, but with that they wish their relations with him to end. In brief, we may say that for near three hundred years our American-English have lived in close contact with the American-African, maintaining towards them an attitude of distinct hostility which is evidently based on a native prejudice against other races than our own. That even when a sense of right-doing has led communities to advocate the advancement of the blacks, it has had no effect in overcoming the deep-seated dislike which is felt towards them.

It must not be supposed that this intense natural repugnance of our people to other shapes and colours of man than their own is entirely base or altogether evil in its effects. It is only a very notable instance of race prejudice such as commonly exists among men and the lower animals towards other varieties of their kind. The Chinese who have suffered from this motive in our country have it themselves in quite as strong a form. Among animals and primitive men this dislike of aliens has a certain advantage in that it keeps the kinds apart, preventing mixtures of blood that lead to degradations. It is, however, unfit that an educated people, such as we suppose ourselves to be, should not have escaped from the evils that arise from their instinctive hatred of other sorts of men. While it is altogether fit and desirable that these aliens should not become united with us in blood, there is every reason that they should be adopted into our society in as large a measure as may be consistent with its preservation.

The most important conclusion that is to be drawn from the peculiar and intense dislike that the English-speaking people, especially the American branch of it, have to alien races, concerns their relations to possessions in foreign countries. Seeing as we do how complete has been our failure to do justice to the Indians, the Chinese, and the negroes who abide with us, we are led to doubt whether we shall prove to be sympathetic or even merciful rulers of other alien folk in remote lands. We may reasonably believe that good as is our quality in dealing with our own kind, we cannot expect to be more successful in caring for distant aliens than we have been with those who dwell with us.

There are yet other qualities which are perhaps as characteristic of our American people as those already noted, though they may be of less importance to the future of the commonwealth. Among these we may mention their inventiveness, their desire for education, and their generous giving for public needs. As for the first of these qualities, it appears to be due to the peculiar conditions of American life rather than to any special gift. All men of our Aryan race are given to seeking for new and better ways of doing things, but their efficiency in this work depends upon the stimulus that comes to them from their surroundings. Thus in the fifteenth and sixteenth centuries Italy, then intellectually as active as our own country is now, produced great inventors, one of whom, Lionardo da Vinci, commonly known as one of the foremost painters of all time, was the father of modern engineering, and perhaps the most original and fertile of all inventors. Yet in the subsequent centuries of intellectual stagnation little in the way of mechanical contrivances has been produced in that country. Our American spirit of invention is to be regarded as a continuation of that of England, but in the results it has gone beyond the mother country or any other.

The value of the inventive motive which so characterises our people is not to be measured by the results in the way of new machines, however important these may be, but is to be found in the manner in which our people deal with all sorts of difficulties. Among uninventive folk the trials that come in their daily round of duty are met in a routine way: they are content to do what their fathers have done under like conditions; any effort to better the conditions is apt to be considered sacrilegious. After a while this form of conservatism may be so fixed that a race once very inventive, as the Chinese certainly were in ancient times, may become apparently incapable of originating anything new, or even of adopting the useful inventions of other folk. Thus the mechanical inventiveness of our people may be taken as a sign of a certain readiness to adapt their institutions and themselves to the varying needs of life, — of a quick adjustment to those changing needs which enables them rapidly to go forward on any path that may be opened to them. It is this quality which, as much as any other, concerns the future of our commonwealth; combined with a desire for the good of his fellows, it should make the American man ready to meet the evils of society and government with a swift efficiency that will clear them away.

In all societies, even in the herds of wild beasts, the safety of the association depends in some degree on the willingness of its members to make some sacrifices for others. In proportion as states gain in true civilisation this willingness to help the common interests increases; in fact, all social advancement depends upon and may be measured by this devotion to the common good. There are many ways in which such work may be done. In ancient times the benefactor commonly gave public buildings, baths, or aqueducts, or strengthened the walls of his city. Later on, in the early Christian ages, much of this effort to help went in founding or establishing monasteries or churches. About five hundred years ago, among the English people, there came a change in

THE AMERICAN SPIRIT

the direction of such gifts, which then began to be devoted to education, to founding public schools and colleges. On the continent of Europe this motive never became general; for a time, indeed, it almost died out in Great Britain; but the colonists of English America brought this motive with them, and have never ceased to be guided by it. In nearly all the thirteen colonies which were joined to form our union of states, the first public work of the people after caring for their churches was to found schools, often those to which they gave the ambitious name of colleges. This same motive has continued at every stage of their advance in the occupation of this continent. Thus when the first Virginian colonists found their way to Kentucky, even before they built their cabins, they provided by law for founding a college.

Not always wisely, but with great wisdom and goodness of purpose, this large giving to the cause of education has continued in this country, and increased from the early days of struggle for existence to our own prosperous age. This mode of giving is, indeed, one of the most characteristic features of American society. It clearly shows that very many of our people feel the responsibility that wealth brings to them, and that they see the clearest opportunity of benefiting their people by helping the youth to a better preparation for the duties of life. This same interest in the generations to come, which is so well shown in many of the exceptionally rich by large gifts to found colleges and academies, exists as well among the masses of our people. This is indicated by their willingness to tax themselves, often heavily, to maintain their schools, not as in most foreign countries, through laws passed by legislatures, but by the action of each school district, where the voters individually feel the burden they willingly assume. Although the proportion of the earnings of our people which is devoted to education varies widely in different states, and much in different parts of most states, it is always large; it indeed much exceeds that which is given to such work in any other country. There are others, as, for instance, Germany, where the work is, on the whole, more effectively done because the control of it is not, as with us, to a great extent in the hands of the people of each school district, but in the central government; yet nowhere else are the objects of education so near to the hearts of men. In no other feature of American life can we find a better augury for the future of our commonwealth than this devotion to the interests of education affords.

The foregoing sketch of the moral and intellectual qualities of the American people needs to be supplemented by a like account of their bodily state. Experience has shown that the folk of northern Europe, whence most Americans are derived, do not do well in all parts of the earth; they have never been successful within the tropics, for in those lands their children are feeble; and the race, except when it is mixed with the natives, soon dies out or becomes much enfeebled in body and mind. In fact, we now know well that the English, Germans, Dutch, and Scandinavians are by nature unfit to dwell in all except the very high parts of the countries lying within about thirty degrees of latitude of either side of the equator, — a realm that contains about half the fruitful lands of the earth; and that something of the same disability, though perhaps in a less measure, affects the peoples of southern Europe. It is, however, now well proved that all the tillable area of North America, from the Gulf of Mexico and the Rio Grande River northwards, is as well fitted for the uses of our race as are any of the countries of the Old World. This is shown by certain facts which are set forth below.

The first settlers of this country came almost altogether from Great Britain, northern Ireland, and Holland. These were followed by considerable numbers of Rhineland Germans, who came here in about 1700, and by some Protestant French. Both these last-named peoples, having been driven from their native lands on account of their religion, were helped to America by England, who at that time was the mainstay of the Protestant Church. The result was, that, up to the beginning of the last century, the folk of this country had been drawn from the most vigorous stocks that man has yet produced, so that our nation began its development on a better foundation of human quality than any other has ever built upon. In the first half of the last century, or from 1800 to the time of the Civil War, there was a large immigration to the United States, much of it from Ireland, which brought us able-bodied men. Though much of this immigration was not good material for citizenship, many were of excellent quality, and the children of all have proved to be of good capacity, so that no reduction in the bodily or mental vigour of the folk came from that addition to the original stock. In the same period there came to us an even greater number of Germans, — people so closely akin to the original British stock that for all the difference of speech they have become effectively a part of our folk.

Since the Civil War there has been a great and unhappy change in the sources from which the immigrants entering this country have been derived. Partly because the Civil War led the English- and German-speaking people to doubt the future of the United States, and to fear that they or their sons would be required to serve as soldiers, they have sought new homes elsewhere. The result has been that the immigrants, though more numerous since that war than in any other like period, have brought us much weaker folk, those less able-bodied and able-minded, less fit material out of which to make citizens, those who have come to us in great numbers from

Russia, Poland, Hungary, and southern Italy. It should be said that some of these immigrants are of excellent quality: they promise to be helpful to the commonwealth and to give us children fit to share with our best in the work of the generations to come; but the mass of these very alien peoples is of a character to make all patriots anxious for the future.

However it may be hereafter, if we continue to permit the lowest-grade folk of the Old World to throng to us, the structure of our American life at present rests firmly on its old foundations of English and other allied folk of northern Europe. These foundations having been laid on a selected body of men and women,—vigorous people, such as alone have the courage and the strength that goes herewith, which was needed to lead them on the difficult ways of the immigrant, — it would naturally be expected that the result of this selection would be a very able-bodied and efficient folk. In many ways this expectation is amply verified. The measurements of the men enlisted in the federal army during the Civil War show that the soldiers drawn from the states, which had received the least number of foreigners since the original settlement in the eighteenth century, were stronger-bodied than the selected troops of northern European states. In the rude tests of war they proved remarkably efficient men. They marched and fought as well as any soldiers of whom we have records. Their endurance to wounds was better than has ever been known in any campaigns. This severe test clearly proves that the American man, born of families that have been in the soil for two hundred years or more, is as strong and enduring as any of his kind have ever been.

To the evidence as to the condition of the body of our American people, which the strenuous tests of the Civil War afforded, we may add that yet better derived from the wholesome work of peace. Our manufacturing industries show that our white labourers in many different employments, probably in all, work more rapidly and effectively and with greater steadiness than those of European countries. They are evidently better adapted to the use of machinery, they appear to be nimbler in the work of hand and mind, than their kinsmen of the Old World. In fact, the present commercial success of this country, a condition in which, with an average wage rate about twice as high as that of other nations, we are able to compete in the world's markets, is evidently in the main due to the fact that our workmen are stronger and swifter than those of other lands.

The fact that our people have gained and are still gaining in vigour, as compared with those of the countries whence their ancestors came, is well shown by the relatively low death rate of the population and the rapid decrease of that rate in the last census, which shows that in a period of ten years the average length of life has increased by about five years. Much of this gain is due of course to the lessened mortality among children and old people; yet it is certain that in this ten years the labouring man of all occupations has won some years more of activity than would in the average have been his in the preceding decade. When we count the costs of the sickness that usually precedes death, it is evident that this gain is worth in money more than all the annual taxes our people have to bear.

There appear to be yet other reasons why the part of North America in which lies the United States should be considered a very wholesome country for our race. Its ancient inhabitants, the Indians, were an able-bodied people who, before the coming of the whites, were remarkably exempt from contagious diseases. So far as can be learned of all the various epidemic diseases, such as the plague, cholera, typhoid, and other contagious fevers, diphtheria, small-pox, etc., which have killed perhaps more than half the people of Europe in the last thousand years, none originated in North America or were known there until imported from the Old World. Moreover, the climate, though in places unwholesome, is on the whole very like that of northern Europe, where our race came to the strength that has enabled it to dominate the world. It affords that combination of summer's heat and winter's cold which insures at once good harvests and a fireside life. There is, in a word, every reason to believe that, so far as the gifts of nature go, our folk have an assured future.

It is well for the dutiful citizen to see that the most certain way to the improvement of the quality of his people is by bettering their physical condition. It is now well recognised that a large part of the drunkenness that curses our society is due to the lack of nutritious food and good breathable air. Certainly a great part of the bodily defects which deform so many persons are owing to insufficient care of children. In a word, the shortest and surest way to a certain gain in the condition of the commonwealth is by improving the ways of living. There is not much chance of uplifting the moral and intellectual quality of the people, except a gain in the condition of their bodies be attained. We see that evident gains, perhaps the greater part of the recent great improvements, come from the instruction which is now given in the public schools concerning the care of the human body. Local boards of health also do much, and should do yet more, to bring people to see what needs be done that they may have health and their rightful share of days. What we have gained in these regards should be but an incentive to push forward in the good work.

CHAPTER XVI

THE FUTURE OF THE COMMONWEALTH

EVERY citizen must expect to hear, and that often, of how the commonwealth in which he belongs is in the course of rapid decay, which will soon end in the loss of its liberties, its good qualities, and its place in the world. Such cries should not vex or make him afraid; they are what have been heard since states began to be. It is said that the oldest-known piece of writing in Egyptian hieroglyphics, set down some five thousand years ago, consists in a lament over the passing of the good old days. It is in the nature of states, as of all else, to die; but this death rarely comes from accident, but rather from the decay of its people, — a disbelief that there is anything in their commonwealth that is worth fighting for. It is the duty of the citizen to believe in the future of the state, and at the same time to strive to make that future what he would have it. It is well for him to remember the excellent story of the men of Rome, who when they were penned within the walls of their city by their arch-enemy, Hannibal, who had overwhelmed their armies in the field, contended at an auction for a piece of land on which the enemy was encamped, bidding for it a higher price than it had brought in times of peace.

Those who decry the strength of the state have their use, as they serve to call the attention of the over-hopeful to the dangers that beset it. It is in the quality of a democracy such as ours that it never in any fixed and permanent way is safe. Other kinds of government may be so formed that they will stand for a long time of their own strength. Not so with our own. It lives with the daily life of the people. When it disappears, it will not pass by slow long-observed decline, or by the assault of some foreign nation, but by a quick change which, while it will leave the edifice appearing to be sound, will yet bring ruin. When the patriotic motive in a majority of our citizens becomes so weak that the state is used for private gain; when the call of duty ceases to move the hearts as it did in 1861, and as it will need to do in many another crisis, — then at once the republic will have fallen: its fragments, even if they be not shared among factions, will not be likely ever to regain its original noble type. Let us understand this sensitive nature of our government and be vigilant in caring for its safety.

The dangers which, in caring for our republic, we have to guard against, may now be briefly considered. The one which naturally comes first to mind is that of invasion by some foreign army. This mischance is most unlikely. Though we are not a military, we

FUTURE OF COMMONWEALTH

are an eminently soldierly, people. It would be extremely difficult for the combined states of Europe to subjugate us. Moreover, they could find no profit in so doing. There is, however, some danger that an uprising of a war spirit might involve us in successive European conflicts which would result in our having to maintain a large standing army as well as a great naval force. The effect of this would be to increase the importance of military men in the state with as a possible result such conditions as exist in the so-called republics of Central and South America, which, as before remarked, are in fact military oligarchies.

There was a time when there was a grave risk that the country would be divided into two nations on the basis of slavery, and of the climate and crops that made that institution profitable. The issue of the Civil War settled for all foreseeable time the unity of this country. Moreover, the land is now so bound together by railways that the people of the different sections each year come into a better understanding with one another.

There is another class of dangers, the nature of which we just begin to see; their gravity we cannot as yet clearly apprehend, though we know that in other lands and times they have proved serious. These arise from the division of the people into classes, — the rich and the poor, labourers and capitalists, farmers and manufacturers, residents of city and country. In a simple democracy such as existed when this country was founded, the employment and resources of the citizens were so far alike that there was no chance for these class distinctions based on various modes of life to arise; but with the increase in numbers and in wealth each day sees them more sharply drawn, and this in a way that appears to many observers to threaten trouble.

If danger comes to us from class distinctions, it probably will arise in some such manner as this: nearly all our people are greatly influenced by the desire for wealth; they judge their government to be good when they are making money, and bad when they are not doing so. They overlook the fact that good times or bad times are generally due to actions over which government has no more control than has religion. They fail to see that about the only way in which the authorities can harm business is by bringing about wars by excessive taxation, or by causing doubt concerning the goodness of the currency. The only way in which they can help it is by leaving men to do their business as they like. Seeing in a blind way that they are not successful in business, the natural tendency of a particular body of folk is to demand what is termed class legislation; that is, laws which will help them at the expense of another group of citizens. If they attain their object they usually find that they are more harmed than helped by the new statutes, but they think that some further addition to their privileges will effect the end. In this spirit we already see the workingmen, as they are called, — the day-labourers of the several trades, the farmers, and other groups of citizens, — organised into guilds which, in form and purpose, are just like those which grew up in aristocratic countries during the Middle Ages; but in a peculiarly unfortunate manner these modern trades' unions tend to set themselves against capitalists with the notion that their ill-success in life is due to the action of those who have succeeded.

It may be granted that the effect of our complicated laws concerning tariffs and taxation has been in a measure to injure men of certain occupations, nor can it be questioned that these men do well to form societies which are to care for their interests. The grave and menacing part of the business begins when one of these groups of people, moved by envy and hatred, sets itself against another in a violent and irrational way. It has several times happened of late that this rage of one class against another has led to armed conflicts which were, in effect, small civil wars; but in each case the commotion has been quickly arrested by the good sense of the other classes of citizens. Yet it seems possible that if the class spirit continues to increase as it has done of late, these accidents may soon be serious.

The only cure for the dangers of the class spirit is to be found in the dissemination of the larger motive of enlightened patriotism. It is inevitable that the interests of particular groups of men should often seem to be opposed one to another, and in some cases really be so. The varying tides of employment and commerce often bring about great and startling changes in the success of various occupations. Thus our farmers recently suffered from a decline of prices which halved the sum they formerly obtained from their grain. This was due to the fact that swift and cheap transportation by railways and steamships brought the crops from realms of fertile land in Manitoba, Argentine and elsewhere, to the markets of Europe. Our iron-makers for the same reason had of late to accept one-half the sum which thirty years ago they received for a ton of iron, and so through the list of earth products. At the same time the progress of invention has cheapened nearly all the products of the factory. In certain ways these changes are to be regretted; they upset trade and lower the rates of payment for labour, but the government can no more cure them than it can droughts.

If the discontented people of this country who have turned to the government for help against the capitalist class have their way, the result of their action can be readily foreseen: they will no sooner begin to receive the help of the state than a struggle will originate in which each group of citizens that is strong enough to influence legislation will have its particular scheme of profit which it will endeavour

FUTURE OF COMMONWEALTH

to set in operation by joining hands with other guilds so as to obtain enough votes for success. Under this system the state will become a mere instrument for creating separated classes, — the kind of government which it was the object of our democracy to avoid. So far as these efforts to obtain such privileges are successfully directed against capital, the result will be destruction in another way: the people who have the capital which keeps the wheels of our great industries moving, and the skill to direct their operations, will begin to fold their tents and slip away to other countries where they may hope to have the equal rights which has been the motto of this republic.

The rapid development of the man of capital in the United States; the process by which hundreds of thousands of able, industrious business men have learned to gather and keep money, — has been the foundation of our prosperity. As soon as these men begin to feel that this is not a safe land for their ventures, they will hesitate to take charge of new enterprises and seek to withdraw from those in which they are engaged. With this state of things the control of commercial affairs will pass into the hands of the weaker men, — men who have not the ability needed to insure commercial success. The results of such action are easy to imagine, but they may be illustrated by examples. Three centuries ago the Spaniards, finding that the Jews were very successful in business, and hating them because of their success even more than for their faith, drove all of that race from the country, stripping them of their goods as they went forth. In consequence of this action Spain quickly lost the control of the commerce of the world and has never regained its place in affairs. In a similar way France forced the Huguenots to leave their country: the exiles bore with them much of the ability of that land to enrich others with their capacity for commerce. It is improbable that the class of men who are or who may become capitalists will be actually driven, in the manner of the Jews from Spain, from this country, but they may easily be led to seek their ventures in other parts of the world where the conditions are more favourable to them. In proportion as this talent for the larger work of industry was withdrawn, the commercial success of the country would be endangered.

The citizen who would preserve the commonwealth from these dangers of class divisions among our people should in the first place strive to increase their appreciation of the unpatriotic nature of the effort to use the government as a tool for private or class advantage. We should urge on them the fact that the only way to maintain the essential freedom of the country is by upholding the principle of equal rights; when that principle is abandoned, the republic is lost.

While it is the duty of the citizen to strive against

FUTURE OF COMMONWEALTH

the dangers of class legislation, as against all those which menace the state, it is not for him to fear overmuch as to the magnitude of the risks which they are likely to bring upon us. He has the admirable consolation of every American citizen that, arrayed with him in the effort to maintain the commonwealth, there is a host of brethren who bring to the service a firm devotion to the principles of true government, and that even those who for the moment are led into evil ways will be ready when the results of their actions are made clear to them to abandon their mistaken course and join with the defenders of the state.

It is characteristic of a democracy where each man's speech is perfectly free that the people express themselves loudly. They often appear fanatical, but all the while there is with them an under-current of sound reason which prepares them in the end to act in a very judicious way. It is this quality that has made the formation and preservation of our nation possible, and it is that on which every patriot may safely rely in his efforts to turn his neighbours to the right way.

INDEX

ABILITY, training of individual, 179 ff.
Abolitionists, 108.
Address, modes of, 17, 18.
Aged, care of the, 198.
American colonies, growth of liberty in, 29 ff.
American history, study of, 51 ff.
American spirit, the, 305-330; fellowship, 309 ff.; pliability, 313 ff.; race prejudice, 316-320; inventiveness, 320; giving toward education, 323.
Americans, bodily condition of, 324 ff.; original stock, 325.
Anarchists, fanaticism of, 105; methods of suppressing, 107 ff.; punishment of, 110.
Anti-imperialism, 255.
Antislavery party, dissolution of, 86.
Aristocracy developed in slaveholders, 225.
Arithmetic, 174.
Arms, citizen's use of, 150.
Armstrong, General, 233.
Assassination of rulers, 106, 109, 117.
Associations for mutual benefit or education, 273 ff.

BANISHMENT as a punishment, 108.
Bankers, 168.
Bible, on creation of man, 6.
Biography is the best method of studying history, 302.
Brute inheritance, 10, 11, 293.

CAPITAL punishment, 125 ff.; state right of, 127.
Capitalist, the, 337.
Catholics as American citizens, 217 ff.
Caucus, the, 80.
Central America, republics of, 65.
Charity law, 129 ff.; and private charities, 131, 195.
Children, the law's provision for, 130.
Church and state, separation of, 216.
Citizenship, the private citizen, 44-63; the practice of, 64-84; party allegiance, 85-102; the law, 120-151; resistance to mobs, 149 ff.; attitude toward complicated questions, 170, 212; distribution of wealth, 152-172; education, 173-184; military duty, 184-191; public health, 191-195; poverty and crime, 195-199; immigration, 200-206; universal suffrage, 206-215; religion, 215-220; negro question, 220-238; foreign possessions, 239-260; city government, 261-271; happiness, 271-279; manners, 279-286; fellowman, 287-300; study of great men, 301-305.

INDEX

City government, and the citizen, 71, 261–271; party politics in, 263; non-partisan party in, 264; lack of interest in, 265; the reformer in, 266 ff.
Civilisation, first steps toward, 16 ff.
Civil-service system, advantages of, 80.
Civil war, political history of, 60; character of the revolt, 135; cause of, 226; results of, 228; fellowship engendered in, 310 ff.; questions preceding and following, 312 ff.; effect on character of immigration, 326.
Class distinctions, 333.
Clubs, 98, 273 ff.
Coinage, 162 ff.
College education, 175.
Commissioners, railway, harbour, and land, 139.
Common law, 121.
Commonwealth, future of the, 331–339; class distinctions in, 333.
Conservative party, 87.
Constitution, alteration of the, 139, 141; its separation of church and state, 216.
Constitutional history, study of, 55.
Cordiality, 281.
Corporations, 133.
County government, 72.
"Court of King's Bench," 121.
Courts of law, 136 ff.; unpopular decisions of, 138.
Criminals and punishment of, 110, 123 ff.; the discharged felon, 197.

DANGERS in republican government, 48.
Dante degli Alighieri, 302.
Darwin, Charles, 3.
Davis, Jefferson, 315.
Death in the animal world, 288.

Death penalty, 125.
Debating societies, 98, 269.
Declaration of Independence, 32; its effect in foreign countries, 33; and foreign possessions, 240.
Defective persons, the law's provision for, 129, 130; individual duty toward, 195.
Degenerate, the, 293.
Democracy, character of a true, 296.
Democratic party, main issues of, 88.
Demonetising of silver, 164.
Discontent in a republic, 209, 213.
Dodge, Col. T. A., 301.
Dred Scott Decision, 138.

EDUCATION, 173–184; through the public schools, 174 ff.; the public library, 179; individual training, 179 ff.; an all-around, 182; through the study of great men, 38, 301–305.
Egypt, foreign rule in, mentioned, 249.
Election debates, 99.
Elizabeth, Queen, attempted assassinations of, 117.
England, colonies of, 53; political parties, 87; administration of foreign affairs, 258.
Evil spirits, 20.

FAMILY, the foundation of society, 17, 66, 295.
Federal government, 78 ff.
Federalism, 87.
Fellow-man, the citizen and his, 287–300; American fellowship, 309 ff.
Flint instruments, 16.
Foreign capital, 160.
Foreign countries, political parties in, 90.
Foreign languages in schools, 175.

INDEX

Foreign policy, 56 ff.
Foreign possessions, 239-260; arguments against, 240, 250, 258; arguments for, 243 ff.; need of, 243; civilising of, 245-249, 254, 320; cost of maintaining, 250; colonisation of, 250 ff.; disposal of, 252.
Fossils, 5.
France, state control in, 134; foreign possessions, 244.
Freedom of speech, 103 ff.; and anarchy, 105, 107; enemies of, 113; limitations in, 115.
Freedom, the limits of, 103-119.
French explorers of America, 52.

GARFIELD, James A., assassination of, 106.
Geography, 174.
George III., 31.
Germans in Pennsylvania, 205.
Germany, foreign possessions, 244.
Gold coinage, 162 ff.
Government, beginnings of, 15-25; local, 65-72; ownership of property, 134, 157; how far it secures happiness to man, 271-279.
Great men, the citizen's study of, 38, 301-305.
Guilds, 273, 333.

HAPPINESS of man and the government, 271-279.
Hayti, republic of, 248.
Health, public, 191-195; care of bodily, 194.
Heroes, study of, 38, 303 ff.
High schools, 175.
History, study of, by the citizen, 51.
Home, the, 66 ff.
Human relations of men, 295-300.
"Hygiene," 193.

IMMIGRANTS, exclusion of certain, 109; probation of, 111; assimilation of, 201; citizenly spirit in, 267 ff.; character before and after the Civil War, 326.
Immigration, 200-206; restrictions on, 204.
Imperialism, 256.
Imprisonment for life, 127.
Income tax decision, cited, 139.
Independence of voters, 97.
India, British rule in, mentioned, 249.
Indians, our relations with, 317; our attempt to civilise, 246.
Individual, development of the, 9, 287 ff.; growth of the idea of, 26, 27; in American colonies, 30; training of individual talent, 179; loneliness of, 294.
Infectious diseases, 191.
Innocent, punishment of the, 124, 146.
Insane, the, 129.
Instruction in principles of government, 110, 111.
Intelligence, origin and development of, 7.
Inventiveness, of man, 16; of Americans, 320.

JAVA, 244.
Jews, religious spirit of the, 306.
Judges, election of, 137.
Jury duty, 137.

KENTUCKY, political clubs in, 98; lawlessness in, 148.
Kings as judges, 121, 145.
"Know Nothings," 274.

LANDSCAPE, beautifying of, 277.
Law, beginnings of, 24; swift service of the, 110, 124; the citizen and, 120-151; origin and develop-

ment of, 120, 143; common law and statutes, 121; criminal law, 123-129; charity law, 129-132; property law, 132-134; support of, 134, 145, 150; revolt against, 135; hasty alteration of, 141; law-making, 142; mob violence and, 146 ff.

Leaders in politics, 211.

Liability of stockholders, 133.

Liberals, 87.

Liberty, what it is, 26-43; its growth in American colonies, 29 ff.; able discussion of, 34.

Libraries, public, 179.

Limits of freedom, 103-119.

Lincoln, Abraham, quoted, 93; assassination of, 106.

Local government, 65-72; compared with state and national, 76.

Lynching, 125, 147.

McKinley, William, assassination of, 104, 115.

Mafia, the, 204.

Magistrates, setting apart of, 118.

Man, physical origin of, 2-5, 13, 287 ff.; spiritual, 7-11, 14, 291; social, 11, 16; his brute inheritance, 11, 293; loneliness of, 294.

Manners of the citizen, 279-286.

Massachusetts limitation of suffrage, 207.

Memorising, 304.

Mexican war, 57, 239.

Military duty, 184-191.

Militia service, 190.

Mob violence, 110, 144-151; savagery of, 145, 149; and the law, 146 f.; as murder, 147; armed resistance of citizens, 149 ff.

Money question, 62, 161-168.

Murder, penalty for, 125 ff.

Napoleon Bonaparte, compared with Washington, 39.

Natural science, study of, 175.

Nature, savages' idea of, 19.

Negroes, their advent in America, 221; capacity for labour, 224, 231; as slaves, 225, 318; as citizens, 229 ff., 247; advancement of, 231-238; variety of original stock, 232; training as artisans, 233, 237; race prejudice, 234, 318; social recognition of, 236.

New England town government, 69.

Newspapers, 101.

Nihilists, 122, 123, 269.

Non-partisan party, 264.

Occupation, choosing of, 180-183.

Office-seekers, 80.

Orator and legislator, 82, 100.

Original sin, 293.

Panics, financial, 160 ff.

Parkman, Francis, 52.

Parties, the formation and dissolution of, 75, 85, 91; the two great, 87 ff.; in city government, 263.

Partisanship, 49, 89, 93-96.

Party leaders, 96, 102.

Patriotism and war, 187.

Paupers, 129, 131, 198.

Pensioning of citizens, 198, 199.

Personal responsibility, 44.

Philippines, 240.

"Plutarch's Lives," 301.

Political clubs, 98.

Political leaders, 211; rearing of, 49, 100.

Politicians, professional, 258.

Politics, avoided by ablest men, 79; and bread-winning, 270.

Polynesians, civilising of, 254.

INDEX

Porto Rico, 240.
Poverty and crime, 195-199.
Presidential bodyguard, 116.
Presidential campaigns of 1860 and 1896, mentioned, 91.
Prices, rise and fall of, 166.
Primitive man, 2, 15-25.
Prisons, 76.
Private charities, 131, 195.
Private citizen, the, 44-63.
Profit and loss, 153.
Prohibitionists, 91.
Property, institution of, 16, 22; government ownership of, 134, 157.
Property law, 132-134.
Property qualification of suffrage, 207.

RACE prejudice, 234, 316-320.
Reforms, 74, 266 ff.
Religion, and science, 6; an attribute of man alone, 7; beginnings of, 19; and patriotism, 42; and the state, 215-220.
Republican Democrats, 87.
Republican government, dangers in, 48.
Republican party, main issues of, 87 ff.; dangers in, 101.
Reversions, 292.
"Ring," the, 80.
Roman Catholics as American citizens, 217 ff.
Royal Commissioners of England, 140.
Russia, anarchists in, 107.

ST. JOHN, Spenser, cited, 248.
Sandwich Islanders, civilising of, 254.
San Domingo, republic of, 248.
Schools, public, training for citizenship, 174; essential studies, 174; school committees, 176; improvement of, 177; and Roman Catholics, 218.
Science and religion, 6.
Shakespeare, William, quoted, 283.
Sicilian immigrants, 204.
Silver, coinage, 162 ff.; demonetising of, 164.
Slave trade, 223.
Slavery, 59, 225.
Socialist, 269.
Society, origin and development of, 15 ff.; is a natural outgrowth of man's development, 35, 295.
Soldier and citizen compared, 45; military duty, 184-191.
South America, republics of, 34, 65.
Southern states, the homes of, 67; secession of, 226 ff.; reconstruction period, 311.
Spanish colonies of America, 33.
Species, origin of, 4.
Speculators, 169.
State government, duties of, 76.
State, share of the average man in the, 44-63.
States' rights, 58 ff.
Statute law, 121.
Stock companies, 132.
Struggle for existence, 3.
Suffrage, universal, 206-215.
Superstition, 20-22.
Survival of the fittest, 3, 9.
Switzerland, republic of, 51, 63.
Sympathy, the basis of true citizenship, 36, 296; development of, 37; need for, 294; crude and harmful form of, 297.

TARIFF, 87.
Teachers, pay of, 177.
Tories, 87.
Toussaint L'Ouverture, 248.
Town government, 68 ff.

INDEX

Trades' unions, 335.
Tribal stage of society, 17.
Trusts, 133.

UNIVERSAL suffrage, 206–215.
Unwritten law, 122.

VILLAGE improvement societies, 193.
Voter, independence of, 97; qualifications of the, 207, 211, 212; neglect of duty, 214; motives of, 214.

WAGE-EARNER, 161, 166.
War, in primitive period, 18, 188; in Middle Ages, 28; financial loss in, 185; moral evils of, 186; idealisation of, 187 ff.; modern, 189; discouragement of, 191.
War policy, mentioned, 113.
Washington, Booker, 233.
Washington, George, compared with Napoleon, 39; foreign policy of, 56.
Wealth, its origin and distribution, 152–172; acquisition of, 153 ff.; government ownership, 157; panics, 159; money question, 161–168.
West Virginia, lawlessness in, 148.
Whigs, 87.
Witchcraft, 21.
Woman suffrage, 212.